The Meaning of Music

Leo Samama

(translated by Dominy Clements)

AUP

First published as *De zin van muziek* (ISBN 978 90 8964 570 8)
© L. Samama / Amsterdam University Press B.V., Amsterdam, 2014

Translated by: Dominy Clements

Cover design: Sander Pinkse Boekproductie, Amsterdam
Lay-out: Crius Group, Hulshout

Amsterdam University Press English-language titles are distributed in the US and Canada by the University of Chicago Press.

ISBN   978 90 8964 979 9
e-ISBN   978 90 4852 892 9 (pdf)
e-ISBN   978 90 4852 893 6 (ePub)
NUR   663 | 665

© Leo Samama / Amsterdam University Press B.V., Amsterdam 2016

All rights reserved. Without limiting the rights under copyright reserved above, no part of this book may be reproduced, stored in or introduced into a retrieval system, or transmitted, in any form or by any means (electronic, mechanical, photocopying, recording or otherwise) without the written permission of both the copyright owner and the author of the book.

Table of Contents

1. By way of a foreword   9

Part A
2. Looking over Franz Schubert's shoulder   17
3. What is music?   27
4. Where does music come from?   32
5. Music as imitation   37
6. Music as language   43

Part B
7. Bach: Prelude in C major   55
8. Music and communication   76
9. Music as notation   84
10. Music as a temporal art   91
11. Music and emotion   95
12. On depth and elevation   102

Part C
13. Beethoven: the Fifth   113
14. Classical music   125
15. Hearing, listening and remembering   131
16. On composing   135

Part D
17. Dvořák and the Bohemian overcoat   149
18. A memorable moment   156
19. The conductor   159
20. The performing artist   172

Part E
21. Lully: the King is dancing	185
22. As the ancients sang	194
23. The history of the history of music	204
24. By way of an epilogue: music now	222
Further Reading	234
Index of names	236
About the author	240

A few words of thanks
This book came about at the request of Maaike Groot, who until 2014 was my enthusiastic publisher at Amsterdam University Press. The Dutch version was edited by Odilia Vermeulen and Ton Braas. Once again, they enabled me to write what I wanted and express what I had to say. I am also most thankful to my colleague Dominy Clements, who translated the text into English.

Voorburg, December 2013 (January 2015)

1. By way of a foreword

This is by no means a textbook, and at most a book to be read for pleasure. In it I have captured some of my experiences while exploring the wonderful world of music. These began when I was about six years old, and my parents gave me an old record player with a few 78 rpm discs. As far as I can remember, these were some Beethoven violin sonatas played by Yehudi and Hepzibah Menuhin, a few of Max Reger's sonatinas with the Dutch pianist Cor de Groot, and Safford Cape with the Belgian Pro Musica Antiqua performing works by Guillaume de Machaut. Apparently my parents were of the opinion that this was a good first selection for a child of six, and indeed, perhaps they unwittingly shaped part of my future. As a teenager I was allowed to sit next to Hepzibah Menuhin to turn pages for her, and as a student I did extensive research on Max Reger and his Dutch contacts for one of my final theses. To this day I am fascinated by developments in the performance of early music, even though my own expertise is based more around 1600 than 1350.

In the same year that I was given the record player and during a hot summer, our opposite neighbour died. She was Alice Heksch, a well-known pianist and one of the first Mozart specialists on the fortepiano, though I knew nothing about that at the time. As far as I was concerned, she was the mother of three somewhat older children, who were often in our house that summer. Their father was the violinist Nap de Klijn. The room in which Alice Heksch lay ill was shielded from the hot summer sun by a yellow curtain that moved gently in the breeze. That summer my parents also played me a long-playing record, *Mozart raconté aux enfants,* on which Mozart's life was narrated by Gérard Philipe, a famous French actor who had died at a young age. This told of Mozart's journey to Paris, where his mother died in 1778, the sad moment unfolding to the first part of Mozart's *Piano Sonata in A minor.* How heartbreaking could you make things for a child? That sonata, the death of Mozart's mother and that of the mother of the neighbouring children behind that yellow curtain have remained inextricably linked in my mind ever since.

The music lessons I had in elementary school turned out to be no less important in my journey through music. We had a teacher who, with a great deal of understanding and attentiveness, introduced us to what music is and, more especially, how we could participate. With her guidance, we performed a children's opera by the Dutch composer Tera de Marez Oyens: *De koning zoekt een liedje* (*The king searches for a song*), and it was thanks to this teacher that I took my first active steps in music. As a result of my recorder lessons with her I was swiftly paired up with her son so that we could play duets together. He was the same age as me, and we soon discovered a wealth of old and new pieces for two recorders. Her name is Marijke Ferguson, and her son is the renowned author Willem Jan Otten. Since those childhood years, my interest in and love for music has always remained.

When I was about thirteen, my younger sister and I took the train every week from Hilversum to Utrecht, where, in the former Institute for Musicology on the Rijnkade, the newly established local Jeunesse Musicale or 'Youth and Music' department had a youth orchestra directed by the young Dutch composer Bernard van Beurden. Here we played tiny 'children's symphonies' that were indeed tiny in every regard, but one day Van Beurden had a surprise for us. He had set up a large blackboard in front of our chairs, on which he had written a series of twelve different tones in musical notation. The intention was that we would improvise with these twelve tones. One of us had to play the whole series, the other only a part. We were free in our choice of tempo, and in the duration of each individual note. Van Beurden led us step by step through this intransigent material, so that after about an hour we began to discover something in what we were doing: a story, our story – and music: twelve-tone music. Ever since that afternoon, contemporary music has been a source of endless fascination for me, even when I haven't always liked what I've heard or played. The path towards writing my own music was paved.

One day, in the sixth class of high school, I was asked by the headmaster to take over the music lessons of the first class. The music teacher was ill, and it might be some time before he returned. I had just been given a beautiful book by my parents, *The Joy of Music* by Leonard Bernstein, and I had also recently seen a few of his *Young People's Concerts* on TV. In short, I knew what to do. I can't remember whether I succeeded, but the experience certainly gave me a taste for teaching, and not long after I started giving Sunday afternoon readings in the Rosa Spier Huis, an exclusive care home for elderly artists and intellectuals in Laren, near Amsterdam. The pick of the Dutch intelligentsia sat opposite me in the small hall, and they took the greatest of glee in rapping me over the knuckles at every opportunity. This was apparently no deterrent, however; on the contrary. As soon as I was given the chance to teach I grabbed it with both hands, and I can now look back on forty years of educational involvement in numerous institutes.

Many of the subjects that have been important to me over the years and the insights I have acquired through doing, reading and learning – sometimes with only a week or two's advantage over my students in the beginning, but later with a little more ease and perspicuity – have found their way into numerous articles and lectures, and also, to a certain extent, into this book. This is therefore above all a personal account, and not an attempt to dish up absolute truths, should they even be said to exist at all. There are few certainties in music. There is, of course, an ever-increasing stockpile of information about the lives of composers and their music. We have endless quantities of scores, and there are many documents about composers and their work that have survived from their own time – documents with reactions, evaluations, theoretical reflections and analyses – but truths? These are rarely to be found.

There are no definitive answers, nor do we have a definitive history. Kant was certainly often right in his in-depth reflections on music, but he also got it wrong. The same goes for Saint Augustine, Schopenhauer and Adorno. Mozart and Beethoven cannot be qualified in absolute terms as the greatest composers who ever lived, and not even Bach can be described as such. They are the greatest in our culture and in our times, and will be for as long as we continue to relate to music in the way we have for the last few centuries. This book does not provide the ultimate answers to so many questions. It contains possible answers, and in many cases no more than my personal answers.

We live in a labyrinthine world; a world in which monocultures barely exist. Mutual influences and fusions increasingly characterise our existence and our ways of thinking. The majority of subjects in this book therefore provide space for a variety of perspectives. In the case of music, the lack of unique or final interpretations is even greater than with the visual arts or in literature. For this reason, I will make no attempt to tell balanced and orderly stories. That would suggest that there is such a thing as a single history of music, and only one view with regard to this most intangible of subjects.

The only certainty that I would dare to advance is that music plays an irreplaceable role for virtually the whole of humanity. We can't do without it. As an expression of what we do and think as people, music, just like painting, literature and philosophy, represents who we are. These things define us as people, and give us an identity. As a wordless language, music is better placed than other forms of expression as a means of communication that can break down boundaries. More than any other form of art, music can also touch us physically with the immediacy and power of pure sound. At the same time, music is more abstract than every other form of human expression, with the exception of certain facets of mathematics and philosophy.

Despite all of the emotions that we undergo when listening, music demands of its participants – composers, performing musicians and listeners – that in the first instance they engage their brains, in order subsequently and on that basis to be able to offer space to their emotions. Music is transformed into such a remarkable phenomenon through a combination of faculties:

the mathematical qualities of an architect, the abstract thought of the philosopher and the communicative gifts of an orator. At its best, music is visionary, earthy and physical, exceptionally complex and deeply contemplative, but it is also very direct. We can listen to it mindlessly and have it hit us with an unforgettable intensity, and in its aftermath become equally fascinated by the logic with which the master builder has erected his structure in sound. For many music is like a belief or a ritual, and for others it offers relaxation. It opens up far horizons and dream worlds, can elevate us from the everyday and, through its directness, also bring us back to the present with both feet firmly on the ground.

In recent decades, complaints have been made about the elitist character of what is popularly referred to as classical music, or the higher art of music. Fortunately a substantial amount of music *is* elitist, in the sense that we look up to it; it occupies an exalted plane above us. It is expressly this exalted, transcendental side of music (indeed, of all great art and all higher thought, both secular and religious) that points the way upwards for us, consciously and unconsciously. Is it not the case that humanity strives to follow an upward path? The more people who feel this desire, and who seek out and act upon it, the fewer there will be who perceive this objective as elitist. It is precisely the task of art as a cultural product to reach as many people as possible and take them along on this upward journey. There can be no concession or compromise. Let the best music remain elitist and let us all, composers, musicians, artistic directors and radio programmers, expose as many people as possible to its exceptional qualities: something to which I hope this book will also make its own contribution.

Part A

2. Looking over Franz Schubert's shoulder

There is a painting of Franz Schubert at work. He sits in his dressing gown, a quill in his right hand. His head rests against his left hand, and there is a pair of slippers on his feet. A lamp shines onto the tabletop, and the shadow cast onto the wall next to him seems like an apparition. Schubert is composing, and there begins the mystery. Composing: how is it done? Cesare Bacchi painted his canvas a hundred years after the composer's death.

1. Cesare Bacchi, *Schubert at work* (1929).

Then, and now, but also in Schubert's own time, the composer's craft was surrounded by riddles: more so than that of the painter, the sculptor, the writer or the choreographer.

Even though Schubert's friends described his work routine in plain language, the questions remained as to exactly how he arrived at those notes, those melodies and harmonies. Did he hear the whole orchestra or the singers singing in his head, or could he feel the piano under his fingers even though there was no piano to be found in his room, at most a guitar? 'Schubert sat at his work desk at six o'clock every morning,' wrote Anselm Hüttenbrenner, 'and composed until one o'clock in the afternoon. During this period a number of pipes were smoked. In the afternoon he went to the coffee house to drink, to smoke, and to read the newspapers for a few hours.'

Schubert didn't use an instrument to compose. Now and again he would check something on a piano elsewhere, and sometimes he might try a few chords on his guitar. He chose to work in absolute silence, as the sound of an instrument would only disturb his thoughts. He would occasionally play his tabletop like a dummy keyboard, just to feel a passage in his fingers, but even if there was noise from outside he would continue undisturbed. The clattering sounds of the street, people talking or children playing, even cold and damp conditions or bad light: nothing could distract him or prevent him from working.

I can't imagine a more perfect image for the lonely creative artist: a man, a quill, a sheet of paper, a lamp, and that shadow on the wall. This is where it all happened, though Schubert also composed while walking around town or in the country, or even while in the pub: always in his head, and therefore invisible to outsiders. A good symbol had been found for this hundreds of years earlier: the dove on Pope Gregory I's shoulder, which gave him inspiration for his ecclesiastical chants. This was what the faithful sought, the Holy Spirit whispering divine melodies into the ear of the Pope. Many people still have this image in mind when it comes to inspiration and creativity: it has to come from somewhere.

There has never been a composer who focused alone on the act of creating, not even Schubert. When a work is ready, it has to be turned into sound: it must be performed, by the composer himself or by others. Ultimately the piece only really exists at that moment, when the musical work of art becomes a listening experience, also for the composer. Very few people are able to read a music score as they would a novel, and therefore have that physical experience, or at least be able to imagine sounds from the page alone. The actual experience can only happen in the reality of the sound, and this is why the practice of music almost always consists of an unbreakable triangle: composing, performing and listening. Each of these has its own rituals, functions, history, position and points of view.

Every one of these three fundamental principles of musical practice also leads to further division and reflection, and in the end to the question as to how we, as creative, transformative and receptive people, can experience music in such an intensive and all-encompassing way, without truly understanding how or why. The mystery remains, whether one composes, performs or listens. Music is almost ubiquitous in people's lives, and probably has been for many tens of thousands of years. We experience the power of music individually and collectively, in concert halls or churches, at a pop concert or dance event, on the football field.

With this, we inevitably arrive at another aspect, namely the function music has in society. After all, as soon as music begins to sound, there are participants in this event. First of all the composer, as the supplier, then the performing musicians and the listeners, and sometimes also the composer as the performer of his own notes. None of these is involved in the performance in a disinterested way; not even the casual passer-by, the unexpected guest or the person who doesn't want to listen at all. Once you hear music there is almost no way of avoiding it. This has to do with what music is, beyond its mere sound. It is what music represents, what listeners make of it individually or collectively, and what music can do with or for us. Music is a social phenomenon.

Let us return briefly to the painting of Franz Schubert at his work desk, since the romantic image of the artist depicted here is a deceptive one. For us, Schubert is still the prototype of the 'free young man' with a great talent. He lived for music. As he said himself, 'I was born to compose and for no other purpose.' Schubert is seen as the bard of country life, of unrequited love, of the desires of the common man, of the beautiful miller's daughter, of winter wanderings: in short, Schubert the dreamer. But is this the truth? Did he really stand so far outside of society?

We do know a few things for sure. During his short life, Schubert did in fact pursue the security of a permanent post. To this end he had studied at one of the best schools in Vienna and with one of the best teachers, Antonio Salieri. His father didn't see a life in music as suitable, however, as the chance of earning a decent living was minimal. He had the career of a schoolmaster in mind for his son, just like himself. The young Schubert was determined to be a musician however, and applied here and there for work, but to no avail. A position at the Opera, to which he presented numerous (not entirely successful) operas, or at the Court chapel: none of these were granted. So it was with reluctance that he became a 'free young man', and while he enjoyed that freedom to the full for as long as his friends were able to maintain him, this was never his aim.

Schubert was never a social outsider, as the image of the 'wandering' composer suggested. He was a social climber. His father had come to Vienna from the Silesian part of Moravia, and his mother was of Bohemian descent. Schubert's parents settled in the northern suburb of Lichtental in the Himmelpfortgrund district. More than three thousand people, the majority of them immigrants, lived there in some eighty new apartment buildings, all of which lacked on-site sanitation. After several years working as a teacher in Lichtental, Schubert's father was fortunate enough to be able to buy his own house and provide his youngest son with a decent musical education. Schubert was well aware of how far he would have to scale the social ladder, given his talent and social background.

Around the age of twenty, Schubert joined the literary clubs of kindred spirits in Vienna and Linz, introduced by friends such as the poets Franz von Schober and Johann Mayrhofer. These were places in which the most recent novels and poems were read. The ideals of the mostly youthful membership were freedom, fatherland and friendship, at a time in which freedom of thought was a scarce commodity under the Metternich regime. In the first half of the nineteenth century, reading clubs were not only in favour as an intellectual pastime, but also as a place where people could meet relatively undisturbed under the guise of art and culture (and a little entertainment), without such meetings being classified as dangerous to the state and therefore forbidden.

Among Schubert's friends in these clubs were supporters of the war of liberation in Greece and opponents of the reactionary and restrictive government in Vienna. Together they read newspaper articles about politics, devoured the latest collections of poetry, and discussed the meanings of these texts in the light of their ideals. With this in mind, we can place many a poem from this period (and even the previous decades) in a context other than the exclusively poetic. There was enthusiastic praise for the freedom of the wanderer in nature, of itinerant singers or street musicians. For this alone, Heinrich Heine was one of the most beloved poets amongst the youth of his time, wandering through nature to express his resistance to the autocratic regime.

People were also still reading the poets of the previous aristocratic era, such as Christian Schubart, whose *Die Forelle,* through Schubert's music, remains a symbol for rural life and romantic charm to the present day. Schubart's poem can also be seen as a warning, however: the freedom of the trout in the stream is short-lived once the fisherman has him on his hook. Neither should we overlook the last lines of the poem, which were ignored by Schubert, in which the trout suddenly becomes symbolic of a young girl, and 'Ruthe' becomes not only a fishhook, but also a rod. Was Schubart talking about dissolute boys who wanted to entrap girls, or might this even be the 'jus primae noctis' to which Mozart also refers in *Le nozze di Figaro*?

We are dealing here with possible underlying meanings, reading between the lines, and perhaps even listening behind the notes. It is precisely this oft-hidden meaning in a work of art that can expose its deeper layers and explain its creation from a variety of viewpoints and extra dimensions. Did Schubert merely write pleasant, folksong-like works in a rural setting, or did he want to point to something that would have been understood by his 'target group' at the time, but that now eludes us?

This applies not only to Schubert and his music: one could say that our perception of the many signals in the works of Machaut, Josquin des Prez, Monteverdi, Purcell, Mozart, Beethoven, Verdi, Bruckner or Tchaikovsky hardly exists today. We are often ignorant of the sources to which they allude. Equally, we do not have the knowledge that would have allowed listeners of the time to understand to what the composer was referring. We no longer have the ears to distinguish the nuances that would then have seemed obvious. We are, for instance, no longer shocked by dissonance, even when it occurs in the 'wrong' place, such as at the beginning of Beethoven's *First Symphony*. Works of art from the past have been removed from their original context, and to us have become more abstract than the composer might ever have imagined.

Are some of Schubert's songs indeed simply the romantic scenes that we like to recognise? Is the *Moonlight Sonata* by Beethoven really a sonata about a loving couple under the light of the moon, or rather an ode to death? After all, between his sketches, Beethoven copied a fragment from the Commendatore's death scene in Mozart's opera *Don Giovanni*: the same triplets, the same lingering pace... And do we have sufficient knowledge and understanding of the melodies of the Church of Rome and their many variants to be able to recognise the references to numerous religious chants in the polyphony of Josquin, Lassus or Palestrina, and thereby to give them their correct meaning?

Are the symphonies of Brahms or Bruckner as absolute and autonomous as we think, or have we become deaf to the secret (melodic or other) messages woven into them, precisely because we want so much to understand the music of these composers as absolute and autonomous? Do we have enough insight into the complex web of textual associations and musical references in the songs, chamber music and symphonies of Schubert to understand them properly, without always associating them with that romantic bard and his delightful, folksong-like melodies?

As I have already said, Schubert's world was much wider than that of the average whistling songsmith. He was well-read, curious, widely orientated, ambitious and especially well grounded. Mozart and Beethoven were both idols of his, and at the same time he had sufficient knowledge of harmony, counterpoint and every important instrument to be able to write a song, a work for piano, a string quartet, a symphony or an opera with equal ease. In the later 19th and first half of the 20th century, his genius was predominantly recognised as that of a composer of songs. Beethoven was his superior in every other genre. The same was true of Schumann, for whom only the great works for piano were above criticism. Neither Schubert nor Schumann sought to compete with Beethoven, however. Of course they wanted to learn from Beethoven, but not to compose as Beethoven, whose aesthetic was not theirs. Where Beethoven thought in terms of tragedy and of ancient drama, the world of Schubert and Schumann was that of the novel, the fairy-tale, the narration of fantasy. This was also the case in their music, and they were looking for other narrative solutions. Both had to shake themselves free of Beethoven in order to become his equal.

Whilst Schumann and Brahms were able to work with some critical distance between themselves and Beethoven, for Schubert, this great figure was a living fellow citizen of Vienna with a huge reputation and a large number of supporters, amongst whom were Schubert's friends. Just imagine emerging from beneath that kind of pressure, an effort made all the more difficult because he cherished infinite respect for the man. When Schubert began to compose seriously as a teenager in 1812, Beethoven was already widely known in Vienna as a great master, and ten years later he had acquired the status of a living legend. Until that time, Schubert had almost exclusively made his name through his many songs. He had also, it has to be said, created a unique place for himself in this way, even though the best-known of these were not at the time considered songs, but rather dramatic scenes.

While Schubert's main talent, at the age of 25, seemed to be writing songs for the drawing room and private circles, his ambition, as we have already indicated lay rather in the composing of operas, church music, symphonies and string quartets. It was a challenge for him to reach a wider audience alongside Beethoven, and to create his own market with a recognisable personal style and technique, not as a clone of Beethoven. However, for a number of reasons his efforts failed to take off around 1822. Schubert was already in difficulties with his life-threatening illness, for which he had been hospitalised several times. He had also failed to complete some of his most ambitious compositional plans, the famous example of which that immediately comes to mind being the *Symphony in B minor*, generally known as the *Unfinished*.

We have to ask ourselves whether the work was indeed unfinished, or did Schubert feel it was in fact complete with its two parts? Both theories can be defended, and there is also evidence for both. The evidence suggesting that the symphony was incomplete includes not only the preserved sketches for a scherzo, but also the unfinished state of various other works written at the same time as the symphony. Backing up the 'complete' theory, there is a text by Schubert in which he writes about a dream that addressed his complicated relationship with his father. In its structure and emotional shape, this text is similar to the two movements of the *Unfinished*. Could this be presentable as proof, or is it more a case of 'wishful thinking'? Either way, this symphony has established itself in our consciousness for 150 years as being in two parts. We know nothing other than that it has two movements, and as a result we are unable to imagine the possibility of a four-movement version.

As a work of art, the *Symphony in B minor* exists, as does every composition, simply in the way it presents itself. The degree of completeness of the two existing movements is so perfect that we are simply unable to imagine an alternative version. With these two movements, Schubert arrived in a world that was not only entirely his own, but one that left its mark right up to the first decades of the 20th century, especially when viewed alongside the *Symphony in C major* from 1825/26, which was completed in a four-movement form. Without Schubert's 'endless' melodies, which are often so easy to sing and which he repeats in their entirety, smoothly modulating through the keys with numerous subtle differences, variations and harmonic nuances: without his gift for great romantic stories about longing for love and nature and about human shortcomings, much of the music of later great masters such as Brahms, Bruckner, Mahler, and even Schoenberg, Berg and Webern, would have been different. Only one other masterpiece had the same effect on the music of the 19th century, and that indeed came from the pen of his revered fellow townsman, Beethoven: his *Ninth Symphony*. This influence was felt not through the famous finale, however, but in those other three movements. Here again, we hear how Beethoven was the composer of tragedies, and Schubert of novels.

What Schubert achieved in the last five years of his life in two symphonies (the *Unfinished* in B minor and the *Great* in C major), in several piano sonatas, in the piano trios, his last string quartets, the *String Quintet in C major* and in the song cycle *Die schöne Müllerin*, is not only a uniquely personal musical language, but also the confirmation that he was capable of creating grand and sometimes extremely complex constructions in sound that are not inferior to those of Beethoven. From this point of view, he was not a composer of songs who did his best to write instrumental music of quality, but rather a master architect of musical structures that are unique expressions of bourgeois culture, and which as a result of their song-like melodies and through their psychological layering and harmonic drama, reveal emotions with which 21st-century listeners can still identify.

Did Schubert put all this together consciously? This is a question that can never be answered. We cannot fathom the miracle of musical creation, and are left merely with guesswork. Schubert indeed had all of the gifts, the perfect technical mastery, an insight into the human psyche and also into his own, a great feeling for drama and the right sensors to give expression to everything which concerns us and makes us emotional in his music. When we listen to his music, we are not listening to a single 'thing', but to a diamond of many facets that reflects the impact of so many dreams and insights. Also reflected is the impact of the wide-ranging results of countless explorations into the composer and his world, and, no less, our own explorations of ourselves and our strivings, we who perform and listen to his works, we who change every day but can see ourselves reflected in Schubert's music; music that is always more than just its sound.

3. What is music?

This is a question that is asked time and again: what is music? In a strict sense, music consists of vibrations in the air that are observed by us and then interpreted as sounds. These sounds play out over time, meaning that music is therefore sound over time. A painting can be viewed at a glance, but not a piece of music. Listening to music takes time, even if it is only a second or a minute. Music is also ephemeral. We can't hold it like a book, a painting or a sculpture, so it is ephemeral over time. This was the finding of the composer Rudolf Escher in 1938 in his excellent essay, *Toscanini and Debussy, the magic of reality* (*Toscanini en Debussy, magie der werkelijkheid*): 'On music rests the doom of transience. It flows, while sounding, and is *over*.' The moment at which you realise that you have heard a sound, a note or a chord, is also the moment that you realise that the sound itself has already vanished, is done with, and that it has already been followed by the next sound or the sequel to that first sound.

 Music, however, is not merely sound over time; that would be too simple. When you listen to music, you experience more than just a sequence of sounds. For some of us, music calls up images, for others, colours or a narrative. Music is frequently experienced as not only spiritual, but also as something physical. How often does it happen that, when listening to music, we can't sit still? Music can keep us from falling asleep. Sometimes you can't put a certain melody, a chord progression or a specific rhythm out of your mind, and often it is a combination of these elements that refuses to let go. The sound of music usually consists of an interplay of rhythm, melody and harmony, but equally of the various timbres of innumerable instruments, and of the endless ways in which these elements can be combined and made to interact. We could add that there are at least as many ways to make this music into sound, to perceive it and to give it meaning.

 Music itself, however, is not merely sound; silence also plays a significant role. Music emerges from silence and ultimately returns to it after it has sounded. Silence in music is also coloured by the ever-changing sound of the music of which it is a part. We therefore shouldn't underestimate the significance of silence, either as a part of the composed sound, or as an independent phenomenon that makes us aware of the quality and content of sound, and consequently also the sound of music.

Music consists of horizontal and vertical elements. Melodies run horizontally, as do sequences of harmonies. We can imagine harmony as a vertical element. When multiple voices sound at the same time, the horizontal and the vertical are brought together: namely, the melodies as separate lines and the combination of simultaneously sounding melodies as harmonies. In a multi-voice or polyphonic choral work from the 15th century by Josquin des Prez, the horizontal elements have the upper hand. As the Dutch novelist Theun de Vries described it so well in *The Motet for the Cardinal* (*Het motet voor de kardinaal*):

> I heard many voices in the choir which appeared to be sung by each as if for himself, which rose and fell along invisible scales over and towards each other, sometimes in pairs, sometimes crossing each other's path like comets, dragging a long tail of harmonies behind them. They kept each other in a floating balance, and despite the most artful entanglements everything was as strong and transparent as a silver scaffold in space.

This is also the case with masters such as Johannes Ockeghem, Jacob Obrecht or Giovanni da Palestrina, and with many generations of composers who for more than two centuries entirely focused their listening experience on following those independent lines, in which the separate voices defy gravity like virtuoso acrobats. By way of contrast, large parts of Igor Stravinsky's *Sacre du printemps* feature pounding blocks of chords that are characterised by a tight, rhythmic pulse. The chain of harmonies proceeds horizontally, but now and then one or more voices go their own way, meandering along text and line, after which each is taken up in the same rhythmic pulse, hopping and skipping, or in a whirling dance.

Composers and audiences have had a great fondness for this simultaneity of line and harmony since the middle of the 18th century; that is, for an interplay of chords that accompany a nice melody. They have tended, as many still do, to prefer a more gallant style to the scholarly. Even so, many composers have been determined to carry on using polyphonic (multi-voiced and thus scholarly) techniques, and to combine these with the homophonic (harmonies that move together rhythmically). Mozart was a master in this, as were Beethoven, Schumann, Wagner, Franck and Mahler. Sometimes a single line can say everything in a piece of music. Other times, a composer needs a multitude of interwoven lines and blocks to bring their sought-for ecstasy to life. And we haven't even started to consider the other elements that contribute to sound: the timbre or colour of the various instruments, both individually and combined, the use of tone duration, dynamics (loud and soft), all kinds of rhythms and accents, and, of course, the tempo, the speed at which music unfurls through time.

Music creates a unique time for itself, and above all, a unique experience of time. A short piece can give the impression of being very long, and conversely, time can fly by in a long work. There is music in which time seems constantly to be changing tack: fast, slow, still faster, even slower; sometimes sharply defined, as is the case with Mahler or Stravinsky, or with smooth transitions, such as those in the piano and orchestral works of Schumann or Rachmaninoff. Time and tempo are suggestive tools for musicians, ones with which they can play. For us as listeners, 'musical' time can often create a feeling of timelessness, by which is meant that we are set free from clock time. However, we must not lose sight of the fact that the time spent listening to a composition is entirely different from the time spent in its creation. What the composer does is mere suggestion, giving the impression that the music was written at the same tempo as it sounds. The reality is more likely to be that of long periods of hard work.

Time and tempo are also not always equal in our listening experience. Fast music can be experienced as slow and vice versa. A fast pulse that repeats the same chord has a different effect from that of a fast pulse with equally swift changes of chord, or a slow pulse with an entirely different chord on each beat. We experience time on multiple levels: harmonic/melodic and rhythmic/metric.

Whilst we have established that music is 'sound over time', music is also manifest in another form, namely as symbols on a sheet of paper, as a score, or in musical notation. The influence that the writing of music has had on our thinking about music is considerable. The direct connection between the invention of musical sounds and their performance has become loosened, and in some cases, even entirely disconnected. The living sound takes on a separate life to that of the inner or imagined sound, the physical experience gives way to an intellectual one; the ears are often replaced by the eyes. Music has become visible. There is even music which entirely consists of visual elements, via a graphic performance instead of audible sound.

Music has become increasingly abstract as a result of notation. This is certainly the case in Western culture, in which over the course of many centuries, oral communication from generation to generation has almost entirely been taken over by writing, and the work of music as a written document has taken on a life of its own. It has become an object. This object, however, is not music in its own right and could never be so, since music has to sound in order to exist. Musical notation is therefore 'merely' a guide or a point of reference. Nevertheless, this object can be considered, reviewed, discussed, studied and performed without any knowledge of the source and origins that are vital to the music itself. Music as a notated object is also by no means unchanging. On the contrary, even the most detailed notation remains a symbolic image of the actual manifestation of music, namely as physical sound.

When all is said and done, all music is dependent on its delivery as sound by way of a performance, and thereby on the people who interpret and perform it, who bring it to life. Music is therefore not only what has been laid down on paper, but more particularly, it is what musicians do with it, collectively and as individuals. The relationship between sound and performance can be very intimate: the creator of the sounds playing their own work. Sound and performance can occur at a great distance from each other, however; for instance, when both the composer and the original performing musicians are dead, and we listen to a 'historic' performance on a CD. Even the experience of that particular performance has almost entirely vanished into antiquity. In the practice of so-called classical music, the physical distance between creation, re-creation and listening has become more important to our musical experience than ever before.

4.   Where does music come from?

In order to understand music better, we have to deal with its origins. How have we arrived at something as ethereal as music? What purpose does it serve, and what purpose did it serve in ages past? Where does it come from – not only in an anthropological sense, but also as part of our daily lives? Did it appear, for no reason, out of nothing?

Philosophers, anthropologists, archaeologists, linguists, sociologists and musicologists have formulated numerous theories on this question over the last 250 years. Did music exist before language, or did music emerge out of language? In fact, to this day we still don't know. It is clear that language and music are closely linked and that from the earliest times they had a common purpose: communication. Not only communication between people, but also with the spiritual world. According to some researchers, however, in the earliest times, music would only have been used for relaxation, such as music for dance, more than likely pepped up with plenty of food and drink; in short, no more than a little icing on the cake of life.

In *The Singing Neanderthals* (2006), Steven Mithen explains that Homo sapiens must have been capable of making a distinction between the communication of emotions and the communication of information. Language was best suited for the latter, and music for the former. Mithen therefore assumes that music serves to disseminate emotions. The question is whether this was true from the very beginning. It is nevertheless striking that he concludes that humans are naturally musical, as has also been demonstrated in numerous research publications by Professor Henkjan Honing from the University of Amsterdam. Humanity is connected to music to a degree not seen in any other resident of our planet. Unlike animals, humans have an inbuilt and therefore natural feel for rhythm. In that sense, we can respond physically to music through dance. Humans can therefore put music to various uses, intentionally or not, whereby it not only supplies a means to reflect our emotions but it can also support and give extra meaning to language and verbal communication.

We will return to the relationship between music and emotion later. It is clear that from the outset, music was used for communication, and not only just between people, but also between humanity and the spiritual world. This may even have been the earliest conscious use of music. Hitting a hollow tree-trunk to imitate thunder, whistling through a hollow pipe or with a blade of grass between one's fingers to tame or to call up the wind: in such ways, music can be used in rituals and incantations. It is highly probable that music soon became connected to specific social classes, each with their own music. This would have meant music for all and sundry to be danced to during festivities, alongside music and dance devoted to appeasing the spirits and gods. This latter category would only have been performed by specialist musicians and dancers who were connected to the priesthood.

Thus music must have had a social function from an early stage, and therefore also a political use: as part of the traffic between individuals and, more particularly, groups of people, and thus between the social classes. Long before Plato and even long before the existence of cities (after all, the ancient Greek 'politeia' (civics) and 'politics' have their roots in 'polis', or city), music was connected to and had its origins in various social classes, and was used for a variety of social goals. In addition, music and dance became inseparable. The ancient Greeks believed that music and dance had been brought forth by the muses, who, from their 'specialisms', were also obliged to bear statements of praise to the gods that had created them. In fact, the Greek word 'mousike' means everything offered by the muses: not only music, but also poetry, dance, and even knowledge.

The principal concern in the relationship between the muses and knowledge was knowing what was still to come as compared to what was in the past. The muses were presented as fortune-tellers, not infrequently with music as a means of bringing the oracle into a state of half-dreaming euphoria. Knowledge of the meaning of science also belonged to the muses. In the ancient world, music was part of the so-called quadrivium (a term that was used as such only from the Middle Ages), together with mathematics, geometry and astronomy. Music was seen not only as a science to be studied, but also as a source of other scientific areas. The quadrivium formed the basis for the study of philosophy and theology. This is one of the reasons why music was considered to be so important by the Greek philosophers, who talked and wrote about it so extensively. Incidentally, on the other side of the world, the Chinese philosopher Confucius also argued that an education without music was impossible. His advice was to start with poems, then knowledge of the ceremonies (the laws and rules on which a society is based), and finally music.

Music and language have been connected to each other from the outset, even though in essence they represent two forms of communication: a concrete language and an abstract language. One language supports the other because, along with rhyme and linguistic cadence, music helps people to remember long texts. This may explain the sing-saying of vast poems such as *The Epic of Gilgamesh* or Homer's *Iliad* and *Odyssey*, but it might also apply to the many long stories that were told at court or in town squares by troubadours from the early Middle Ages. We can safely assume that the singing of narrative liturgical texts, in recitative and with an emphasis on the text, grew out of such traditions.

These anthropological sources of music have yielded many wonderful myths since time immemorial, yet there is a source that is much closer to us and which is in fact a part of ourselves: our own bodies. To a great extent, music arises in our bodies; after all, we are the ones who make music. Or could it be that we receive music; should music be understood as a gift? In both cases we have to ask ourselves, where and how does music originate? For instance, can we point to the place where inspiration germinates? Even when we claim that someone has music in their toes, that they make music from their heart or with their soul, or that they make music from their guts (Schopenhauer sited the source of all music in the 'Urwille', where humanity maintains itself as a species), the source of all music is in fact to be found in none of these places, but in the brain, where the signals in our bodies are stored and coordinated and given meanings such as pain, itching, butterflies in the stomach or agitation.

Yet at the same time, music comes from outside our bodies. We can hear, for instance, when someone plays an instrument or sings: the music is delivered *to* us. We are aware of the world around us through our senses. We perceive and hear sounds, see objects, feel, smell and taste. I will go into this further in a subsequent chapter. For now it is important to recognise that music is both within our bodies and beyond, in a constant interaction between the internal and external, and that it can enter, inspire, obsess and enchant us. Creating music is a combination of signals from outside and signals from within.

In addition to this, we have to be aware that music does not only manifest itself as sound. This brings us back once again to the mystery of inspiration, which was already discussed in the chapter on Schubert at his writing desk, and which for thousands of years has been one of humanity's riddles. Is it the muses who inspire us, or the spirits of nature? Is it the dove on Gregory's shoulder (see fig. 2) or is it the song of Orpheus with his lyre? Is the inspiration of music purely that of sound or is it a more abstract thought? Is it an image, or colours? Is it spiritualism or theory, language or emotion, movement or idea, taste or aroma? Maybe it is a mixture of many things, but in order to understand this better, we have to penetrate the human brain.

2. *Pope Gregory I*, 10th century, ivory, Kunsthistorisches Museum, Vienna.

5. Music as imitation

Let us first imagine how it would be to be entirely unaware of the world around us. This may sound somewhat hypothetical, but nevertheless, imagine that none of our senses are functioning. We can't see, feel, taste, smell or hear. Nothing that exists beyond our bodies can penetrate into our consciousness, because no signals are being passed through to the senses. We are like a hermetically sealed pot, a so-called 'monad'; a thing with no windows to the outside. At the risk of tautology, we can use the term 'windowless monad'. The founder of monadology was the 17th-century philosopher Gottfried Wilhelm von Leibniz. He is of little importance to music other than that as a real child of his time, he considered music to be a form of mathematics; a mathematical exercise, to be exact. In his opinion, the pleasure that we derive from music comes from unconscious counting: music and mathematics as allies.

Having established that nothing can penetrate a monad or an insentient person, the question arises, would the inner world of this person contain any form of music? Leibniz was certain that whatever was ingrained in a person's system had to be something pious. These days, we would be highly sceptical of such thoughts. Nevertheless, whereas fifty years ago we still believed that people were mainly formed by their environment and by their surrounding culture, we are now inclined to attach more importance to our physical nature as a result of discoveries about human DNA, and thus to the genetic and physical core of what we are. Is music also a fixed part of our physical system? Is music the result of 'culture' or 'nature'? Or is it not the music itself but our abilities in music, the quality of being musical, which is written into our DNA?

Let me rephrase the question. Would music exist somewhere in our bodies if none of our senses worked? And if this could be answered in the affirmative, which sounds might be present in these darkened vaults that are sealed from the outside world?

First of all there would be the beating of the heart, and alongside that, perhaps, the rushing of the blood and maybe a very high tone coming from the electricity of our nervous system. It remains to be seen whether we could perceive these if we were entirely deaf, but in any case, these are the sounds that we carry with us from the start. Everything else, every other sound, has to come from the outside world. It exists only when it can be heard and, through the grace of our consciousness, by the awareness of each individual. Sounds from the outside world enter our inner world via our senses, coming in especially through the ears. There are also sounds that we can feel through their vibrations, so we become aware of a world of sound around us through listening and feeling.

Due to its construction, the ear is not unconditionally capable of giving us the sounds of the entire outside world. The tympanic membrane in our ear is the first to receive sound in the form of sound waves. For clarity's sake, we can best compare this membrane to a miniature drum. Although the evidence is not watertight, it is increasingly presumed that the eardrum has a strong kinship with a real drum. Thus, its natural qualities may already bring a certain hierarchy to the signals received. The sound waves that enter the ear are therefore not only converted into electrical pulses, but are also filtered. We cannot hear everything that sounds outside our bodies. You only have to think of those dog whistles which are too high for us to hear, or of the very small intervals made in birdsong which we can barely perceive, or not at all.

Every sound that comes in is transformed by the ear in its function as a kind of modem (modulator-demodulator). The outer world and the inner world, however, remain strictly separate from each other. It is not the sound waves that reach our brain, but their translation into electrical pulses, which are only given meaning once they have penetrated our inner world: our consciousness. As a result, all music is not itself but, once it has arrived in our inner world, an image or an imitation of itself.

The outer and inner worlds therefore remain on two sides of our senses, but the one can shine light on the other and vice versa. Our consciousness in the inner world is fed with information from the outer world via filters, which we call senses, and the outer world exists for us only because it is being passed on to us and enters our consciousness through these senses. With our consciousness, we determine what we recognise in and of the outside world, and where and how we place these outside elements and give them meaning.

That the music in our inner world would not exist without a consciousness of sound outside our bodies, organised or disorganised, does not imply that our awareness of music is the result of our consciousness of merely its existence. After all – and I have already indicated this in passing – the sounds that exist outside us derive their meaning from our consciousness, from the fact that we can give meaning to them, that we can also communicate that meaning to others and therefore contribute to a collective consciousness and a collective sense of purpose with regard to the sounds being heard.

Perhaps we should indeed compare the brain with Plato's famous cave, on the walls of which the sun projects the significance of the idea of every single thing. Thus the form of a cow, as an idea of all cows together, is projected on the wall by the sun. In this way, we can use the idea of a cow to recognise every real cow for what it is. If, however, we were to turn and look into the source of light to see 'the' cow, we would be blinded by the sun. Thus it is that the idea of the sound of music outside us turns only into a piece of music in our consciousness when we can perceive it in a sensory way and give it a place in our awareness. In the world of sound this is even a double action, since the written score of the musical thought is the first translation, and the performance of that score the second.

What we understand as music is thus coloured by our consciousness and therefore a meaningful imitation of sounds from the outer world, an *imitatio della natura* of our own physical nature (the hearing organ which determines what we can and cannot hear), of human nature (for instance, the awareness of others), of the physics of nature (the sound waves and the electric pulses with which they are subsequently introduced into our bodies) and of a cosmic or divine nature (for those who believe that our inner world and the outer world possess parallel logical, primordial or divine laws). Even our system of scales and the harmony of tonality can be regarded as examples of *imitatio*, namely, of the harmonics or overtones built into each individual tone, and which are a part of its nature.

Plato viewed music as an imprint of the laws of nature in our spirit. He thought of music as a combination of sound and spirit, both of which, in turn, possess underlying ideas. Every extension of this is no more than an addition. Order of rank, structure or symbol: each is merely a colouration of actual music, of the 'idea' of music. These are colourful additions made by our consciousness on the basis of assumptions. We call these 'hypotheses of consciousness'. We assume that the outer world is the same as that which is shown to us through our senses. Epistemologically, however, these are not experienced facts, since there is no way to test them. We have to trust that our senses are doing their job well, but we cannot in fact be sure of this.

The experiences that we gain in the traffic between the inner and outer world provide us with patterns that allow us to move closer to the world beyond us, and acquire more certainty about how we think the outside world appears and how it connects to each of us. It is these experiences that enable an artist, for example, to find better and more effective ways to realise his ideas. However, the platonic ideas themselves and the ideas of the artist's musical dreams, will *a priori* forever remain just that: ideas.

Music is thus doomed to remain an imitation. Indeed, everything that a composer hears inwardly is no more than an activity of consciousness based on material that first must have been available in the outer world, both acoustically and abstractly (such as the activities of other individuals that have reached our consciousness aurally or in writing). This material is subsequently provided with content of consciousness, and is added to and stored with our own stockpile of information. This results in our brain having an image of the world outside us, and therefore also of the music outside us. That which has settled in and been coloured by our brain is then given meaning. In short, the consciousness of the initially still-'empty' interior world of our brain needs the outside world to provide content, and therefore not only awareness of the outer world, but also of itself.

Thus the dark vaults of a 'windowless monad' need first to be 'opened' and then fed with signals, with observations from outside. These signals can be extremely diverse. They consist not only of the evidential: things that are seen, heard, felt, smelled or tasted, and which provide awareness on the basis of the aforementioned 'hypotheses of consciousness' content. Such signals can also be those that have already been processed by other individuals and which have already been given content by them, or can even be mere opinions or theories, and therefore content of consciousness in their own right. In other words, we build a very complex web of content of consciousness that can also contain its own interrelations. We experience the latter as associations.

On the basis of everything that is offered to (and not through) our windows and is then transformed in order to be able to enter our brain, and which then within our consciousness brings about no more than changes to our consciousness, every individual constructs his hypothesis of the outside world, consciously or unconsciously. It is precisely for this reason that this outer world is of the utmost importance to the study of everything created by humanity: everything that has been thought (philosophy, theology, art, science) and everything that has been made (objects). Even for the creation of the most beautiful music, the composer is in reality 'given' the necessary building blocks. This is not a mystical or religious observation, but one grounded in the philosophical theory of knowledge.

It can therefore be said that a composer is in fact a composite of what lies within his consciousness, which in turn wouldn't exist without his fellow people, his society, his and other cultures, his faith, and even numerous things of which he is entirely unaware but which form him as a person and, piece by piece, contribute to that fascinating and complex play of combinations on which he reports through his music. This is done by translating music into symbols, or directly in a live performance. What is served up to the listener is therefore a make-believe world, a platonic imprint of the contents of the composer's consciousness, and indirectly of his society and his culture, translated into the sounds of a performance and therefore also coloured by the world of those responsible for that performance.

This insight cannot solve the mystery of artistic creation. We still do not know how Mozart or Schubert, Purcell or Verdi, Machaut or Boulez composed, where their musical ideas came from, why inspiration at a certain moment generated that specific result and not a different one. Composers themselves often don't know why, when at work, a particular melody, a certain sequence of harmonies or a particular timbre comes into their head. The only things we know for sure is that composers have to work hard and have an exceptionally large knowledge of every facet of their profession in order to give durability and meaning to their ideas, and that they cannot 'exist' without the world around them, without losing their role as individuals amongst people. In order to understand the background to their music, we must therefore also examine the world that surrounds them, and not only the works themselves.

6. Music as language

Although strictly speaking, music consists exclusively of sounds, it can equally be seen as a language, comparable to our spoken language but composed of sounds: a wordless language or, to formulate it more elegantly, a non-verbal means of communication. In a piece of music, as in a discussion, signals are sent and signals are received, but music cannot transmit concrete linguistic meanings. 'Shall we get a cup of coffee?' cannot be expressed through music. In that sense, music is not connected to the concrete world of things. Music cannot express 'tree', or 'cow' or 'square' or 'circle'; at least, it will not be able to do so for as long as we avoid making music into a language with its own grammar as it applies to spoken language, and as long as we agree not to set meanings for a particular harmony or a particular sequence of tones.

Something along these lines has been tried in the past, such as in the musical rhetoric of the 17th and 18th centuries, but musical language has never achieved an unambiguous interpretation. Users of this language have often resorted to generalities: a descending chromatic line for suffering or death, the crossing of voices for the crucifixion of Christ, certain harmonic twists that might be interpreted as punctuation (a comma, a dash or an exclamation mark), but music still cannot express 'tree' or 'circle'. *The Moldau* by Smetana doesn't portray a river, however strongly that is suggested by the title. Anyone who hears Smetana's music without further explanation might imagine anything which moves up and down or back and forth: trees in the wind, clouds in the firmament, waves on the sea, and, of course, the water of a river. But it *isn't* a river; it can at best suggest a river. We still need the language of words to guide us towards those thoughts.

In fact, the sounds that make up a piece of music are meaningless: pure sound waves that belong in the field of physics. As listeners, we can give meaning to these sounds or sound waves.

As part of this, every transmitter of sounds and every receiver has their own thoughts and intentions. With words, we can give direction to these intentions, and suggest more than we actually hear. However, it is the case that the composer and listener, that is to say the transmitter and receiver, remain eternally on two sides of a dividing line that consists of a complex system of hearing, listening, association and interpretation. We can hope that these two understand each other a little – transmitter and receiver, composer and listener – but even then, the music made by one and heard by the other doesn't really bring the two closer together. The one who hears, listens, associates and interprets will always do these things differently from the other, be they the composer, the listener, or a performing musician.

The consequences for the wordless language of music are clear, given the large number of misunderstandings that can already arise from words and language in daily use. Nevertheless, it cannot be denied that large groups of people experience goose bumps at Puccini, are shaken from their seats by Mahler, go through heavenly moments listening to Mozart or Bach, cannot sit still during the finale of *Daphnis et Chloé*, wave candles or lighters as one at pop concerts or become emotional at hearing their national anthem during awards ceremonies at international sport events. This collectiveness indicates that greater forces are at work here, in which music plays a significant role. It also shows that the group experience is at least as important as that of the individual.

This certainly has to do with the aforementioned physical experience that we have when listening to music, but also with musical encoding or formulas in music that can be interpreted by the listener in a linguistic way (for instance, sequences of harmonies which – as has already been said – have the same effect as the punctuation in spoken language). It also has to do with the multitude of underlying associations that colour our reception of music, individually but also collectively. Even those who have no grounding in music theory can hear when the tempo accelerates or slows down, when the colour in groups of chords becomes less rich, or when it becomes more or less euphonious, more or less dissonant.

When music is constructed on the basis of a fixed system of harmonies, melodic lines or rhythms, every change within that system is noticeable to a greater or lesser degree. This also applies to unexpected accents in the music or changes in tempo (acceleration or slowing down). It is exactly these ear-catching aspects that are perceived and interpreted as meaningful signals. Music has functioned in this way for many centuries, both amongst experts and non-experts, to use the words of Mozart's father, Leopold. Although it is still impossible to talk in absolute terms about music as a concrete language, semiology and music can certainly offer each other a handshake.

The language of words has another relationship with the language of sounds, namely in the way writers and composers tell their 'story'. This is told metaphorically, in communication with another, even when the other is an abstraction. Not only the way in which musical phrases or sentences are built up, but also how they have to be performed is linguistic to a high degree. This can be heard in the way one sentence leads to the next, and how these sentences together tell a coherent story. Musical sentences are connected to each other in the same way. Of course, numerous composers have chosen to base their story purely on more abstract theological or mathematical rules. Even then, we can generally state that the first duty of the performing musician is to seek the narrative and the world of ideas behind the notes, even if these ideas are not the composer's but his own. This is an effective way of creating swifter communication with the listener.

This is not only true of instrumental music; in vocal music, the meaning of the text on which a piece has been composed must of course be communicated, but also the tones, melodic lines and harmonies. As soon as words are used, diction, pronunciation, the sound of the vowels and consonants play an important additional role in the ways in which the purely musical elements should be presented. The language of words and the language of sounds work together, even though they may not always tell the same story. The inevitable question is thus which has the upper hand, the words or the notes? Which is subservient, the prose or the music?

In centuries past, swords have frequently been crossed over the question as to which has the greater authority: the music or the word. This is the case both in an absolute sense – the word as part of our written and spoken language and music as a system of sounds – and in a relative sense, namely in the interplay between language and music. In around 1600 there was even public discussion about this, when the music theoretician Giovanni Artusi accused the composer Claudio Monteverdi of giving more importance in his new madrigals to the words he was setting to music than to the true 'nature' of the music itself. Monteverdi believed that the word should be the master of harmony and not its servant. The music should support the word and give it extra meaning. In that case, you might think that one should listen to the poetry in the first place, and then to the 'accompanying' music, but is this true?

When words are used in a composition (in a song, cantata, oratorio or opera), one might wonder how communication is established: by the words or the notes? After a song recital, do we leave the concert quoting lines of poetry by Goethe or Baudelaire? What about the songs of Leonard Cohen or Bob Dylan, Jacques Brel or Tim Minchin? The underlying question is, when do we remember the words more, and when the music? Don't they both have equal value? Would a song written to a poem by a famous poet be better than a song on the words of a lesser poet? To put it another way, would a song by a lesser composer become better if the verses of a great poet were used?

In the 18th century, such questions led to the statement 'Prima la musica e poi le parole' (which also became the title of a rather nice opera by Salieri): first the music and then the words. This may have seemed logical to the majority of composers, but not all poets were in agreement. This is why Goethe, who incidentally had a good grounding in music, had a low opinion of composers whose music undermined the connotations and content of his poems. This had nothing to do with ignoring the rhyme or metre of the words. He was mainly annoyed when the core idea or *Gehalt* was missed, particularly with songs in which the music went entirely its own way and therefore neglected the form and meaning of the poem. It was his opinion that music supports the poem, and was therefore the servant of the text and not its master.

With this vision, Goethe had a good understanding of the power of music. Music can steal a text away and chase it entirely out of our minds. From their own experience, however, many a composer will also agree with the prolific American song writer Ned Rorem, who argued that in order to write a good song, you must be brave enough to break the bones of the poet: at least, when as a composer you want the music to prevail over the words and to reflect as much as possible what is unsaid; to express what is hidden behind the words. A younger contemporary of Goethe, the novelist, poet and composer E.T.A. Hoffmann, believed music existed in a separate domain from words; that music began where words end. In a way, with this thought, he allied himself with the philosopher Immanuel Kant, who had concluded that music stands apart from the concrete world, and that it therefore cannot be enjoyed on the basis of logic or knowledge.

According to Kant, the strength of music is that it can induce a feeling of well-being, 'a feeling of being healthy'. This concerns the sensual experience of music, that of the senses and not of the intellect. What you can no longer access with your mind or with words, music can make comprehensible to your feelings. This is why music was driven out of the domain of the intellect for a long time, and why the linguistic qualities of music quickly became the subject of a discussion about the degree of abstractness of music. Is it possible for music to express things that can also be conceived in words? Some composers claim this to be so, others deny it. The former are of the opinion that music creates its own language within its own terms of reference; that it is purely introspective and is exclusively about itself. The latter consider music to be directly connected to the linguistic or concrete worlds, and believe that it should be able to give expression to these.

I want to reflect one last time on the relationship between music and language, but then with reference to the time before Palestrina and Monteverdi. From the beginning of the 14th century, composers were looking for a better relationship between words and music. The neo-platonic thought that the 'idea' in music inevitably had to be a divine idea, whereby the theological foundations of music were considered more important than the 'expression' of the word, was gradually enriched with the perception that the music of a song and even that of a liturgical composition could be better attuned to the chosen words. A parallel can be drawn here with paintings, in which painters only began to experiment with the *imitatio della natura*, a certain feeling for realism in the images, in the course of the 14th century. In music, this initially concerned improvements in the connection between the rhythm of the words and that of the music. Not long after that, the meaning of the words became involved. One cannot deny the difference between an *Ave Maria* and a *Dies irae*, between a song of lost love and one about the heroic acts of a brave Knight.

In order to bring the diction of language and the rhythm of music closer together, it was necessary to adapt and broaden musical notation techniques, so that composers would be better able to represent flowing lines and rhythmic nuances. This resulted in mensural notation, in which the duration or mensuration of individual tones could be indicated to the finest degree (see fig. 3). Polyphony became increasingly valued and fashionable in the 14th century (something that had its parallel in the ornate decoration of Gothic cathedrals), while at the same time the neo-platonic theological idea of the *imitatio della natura* shifted more and more to an *imitatio delle parole*, by which composers in the

3. Jacques Barbireau, five-part *Kyrie* from the *Missa Virgo Parens Christi*, Bibliotheca Apostolica Vaticana in Rome, beginning of the 16th century – an example of mensural notation. To the top left is the *superius* (the highest voice), below this on the left on a single stave the tenor, and below that the *bassus* (the lowest voice). To the top right is the countertenor (the low voice directly above the tenor) and below this on the right the *bassus* tenor (the voice directly below the tenor).

16th century tried to capture every single nuance of the meaning of a word and the feelings behind it. The results of this development can be followed more easily in the secular madrigals and chansons than in the liturgical works of the period.

Traditionally, the Church had been wary of too much earthly emotion. In spite of this, liturgical works in the course of the 15th and more especially in the 16th century also became noticeably more detailed in their diction, and more effective and direct than in previous centuries. This is one of the main reasons that after 1560, the Council of Trent made a stand against musical excess and an overabundance of harmonic colourations during the liturgy. This led to a significant retrenchment. The underlying desire in this musical counter-reformation was a return to the word itself, preferably without any distracting music being performed in church. The latter was clearly a step too far, but church music became austere and there was a re-orientation towards unison chants. The word had once again regained the upper hand.

In the last decades of the 16th century there was also a change of direction in secular music. If music can illustrate a text, then the singers in a vocal polyphonic composition are the communicators of that text. The question is, which 'spirito', which voice, do you need to follow in a polyphonic work to experience the intended communication of feeling? Those few brief moments of vocal unison in a chanson or madrigal are no solution. In this way, the ideal of a perfect relationship between words and music, the ideal that in music had led to the Renaissance, was fulfilled by the emergence of a new form of monody in the late 16th century, in which one or two singing (and later also instrumental) voices were accompanied by harmonious chords. This rise in monody, however, launched the Baroque.

Up to the present day it has been found, time and again, that when the emphasis in the relationship between language and music is placed on language, music has to contain itself. Once music becomes complex and idiosyncratic, it takes away the hegemony of language. This applies to liturgical music, to operas and oratoria, to songs and chansons and even to pop music or music for advertisements. There is no more dangerous medium than music: before you know it, the words are playing a merely subordinate role.

To conclude, there is one more interesting question that I would like to raise regarding the relation between music and language: to what extent does language dictate the way in which music is performed? From the point of view of the music, we are indeed inclined to make the words subordinate to the expressiveness of the music, which includes the beautiful sound of singing. Here I am not talking only about opera, in which there is always much emphasis on 'bel canto', or beautiful singing. During their training, singers learn that words can be understood even in difficult passages by using the right colourations of the voice (that is, in the vowels), and a proper articulation of the consonants.

Nevertheless, our experience in the concert hall, at song evenings, at the opera or at performances of choral singing is all too frequently that not a single word of the text can be understood. Singers are not the only ones to blame for this. Sometimes, when writing vocal music, composers also barely seem to take the intelligibility of the text into consideration.

In spite of this, the way in which beautiful melodies and expressive sounds increasingly took the upper hand in the course of the 19th century had consequences that can be considered drawbacks. The real value of music is precisely that it transcends the language of words. That was what people thought then, and what many still do today. This does not mean, however, that music should cover up the words. In many vocal works, the most beautiful and meaningful texts are pushed away and masked in favour of gorgeous singing. This situation is less common in the majority of pop music, chansons, political songs, musicals and folk music. The importance that has been attached to the intelligibility of texts here has long been a part of classical music as well. This is my conviction, even though it has to be based on second-hand reports and discussions about the relationship between language and music, as described above. Since evidently no sound recordings before 1900 exist, we lack examples in sound by way of evidence.

Why should the need to understand the words of a song by Andrew Lloyd Webber be greater than for an aria by Mozart, Verdi or Richard Strauss, not to mention the extensive art of song in the 19th century? Schubert and Debussy actually wrote songs in a similar vein to artists such as Jacques Brel, Barbra Streisand or Herman van Veen, each of whom believed that every word counts. In Bach's vocal works, the words are also at least as significant and substantial as the music. And what about the many masses, motets, madrigals and chansons from the 15th and 16th centuries, in which the composers made so much of an effort to bring text and music into one line, so that the notes fit seamlessly with the words, and so that the diction of the text is fully supported by the music? We should surely be able to follow the words in these?

One would imagine that a composer who uses a text first 'tastes' the words through and through, deciding on the correct tempo for good diction, where the accents lie, where the language rises or falls, how the sentences sound best with the correct punctuation. If the language of the chosen text is also the composer's mother tongue and one he has mastered thoroughly, it is not unlikely that the musical sentences will be written in the same way as the language would be spoken, if necessary bearing in mind the local dialect that he would have used. When we connect language and music one to one in this way, and try to bring both entirely into balance with each other, this can have a significant impact on the manner of singing, and also on the ways in which the punctuation and sound of the language give direction to the music.

Who knows: perhaps then we would be better equipped to understand why purely instrumental music has such an important linguistic content, with sentences and punctuation, and with melodic twists that at times seem noticeably to resemble spoken language. In this manner, music and language are connected to each other on multiple levels, from the origins of their existence to the most sophisticated compositions, from cavemen to John Adams and Amy Winehouse.

Part B

7. Bach: Prelude in C major

In 1722, Johann Sebastian Bach published a volume of compositions entitled *Das Wohltemperirte Clavier*. On the title page he provided a brief explanation of the contents, namely 'Preludia and Fugues in all *Tones* and *Half tones*, both in the *major keys*, according to the *Do Re Mi*, as in the *minor keys* of the *Re Mi Fa*. Written for the utility and use of the studious *musical* young, but also for those who have already achieved proficiency in this special pastime'. Thus the volume consists of two groups of twelve pieces, each divided into a single prelude followed by a fugue, covering all of the major and minor keys. It is also an educational collection, and a way to while away the hours in a pleasant and instructive fashion.

Bach demonstrates numerous ways of writing preludes and fugues. He never repeats himself; not in the preludes, with their many playing techniques, nor in the many-layered fugues, in which voices imitate, mirror and chase each other, sometimes fast and then slow, but always with taste, insight and expertise. Every prelude can be seen as a kind of intonation before the fugue: the tone and atmosphere of the fugue is presented, varied and sparred with. In this way, the mood and attitude of the listener and the musician are prepared for the subsequent fugue. Bach brings in many performance techniques: broken chords, shuttle figures, virtuoso passages, arias and so on. Sometimes the music is open and clear, at other times, complex and intensely wrought.

The title page of the first book of *Das Wohltemperirte Clavier* shows the year 1722. For a long time after Bach's death, the story went around that he had written the entire volume in Weimar or in Carlsbad out of sheer boredom and through lack of a keyboard to play on a daily basis. However, it has generally been accepted that he used existing work as a starting point for part of the first set of pieces, finally bringing these together with the necessary additions, adjustments and extensions into a volume in 1722. In itself, at that time it was not unusual for a composer to recycle his works. The 'unique' work of art that we like to see today is a 19th-century idea. Even if Bach's music is unique and distinctive to us, he would have seen himself as a craftsman who was plying his trade; and who honed, kneaded and polished his products and, where necessary, adapted them for re-use.

This can be seen, for instance, in the match between eleven preludes that Bach wrote around 1720 in the *Clavier-Büchlein* for his eldest son, Wilhelm Friedmann, and the preludes in the first book of *Das Wohltemperirte Clavier*. It is not unthinkable that he was toying with the idea of composing a cycle of preludes and fugues at a much earlier time, even before he moved to the court in Cöthen in 1717. Such collections were not unknown in the first decades of the 18th century. In 1702, Johann Caspar Ferdinand Fischer collected twenty preludes and fugues in almost every key (with the exception of D-flat major, B-flat minor, E-flat minor, F-sharp major and G-sharp minor) under the title *Ariadne musica neo-organoedum*. In 1719, the theoretician Johann Mattheson brought out his study book *Exemplarische Organisten-Probe im Artikel vom General-Bass*, undoubtedly on the basis of years of experience, in which, as the title indicates, all 24 keys are represented – twelve in major and twelve in minor – in simple and difficult exercises.

Those who now compare Bach's music with the aforementioned collections will experience the same feeling of euphoria as those who, after many years slaving over Carl Czerny's etudes, suddenly discover those of Chopin. Not only was Bach capable of connecting the technical study of keyboard playing with the theoretical knowledge of composing, but his music also goes far beyond the level of most of the study material of his time by creating a kind of musical game that anyone eager to learn will find impossible to relinquish.

Of the 24 preludes and fugues in *Das Wohltemperirte Clavier*, we will examine the first prelude (BWV 846:1) from the first book. This short work is a little gem with surprising facets. Before going into this music more deeply, I recommend that everyone

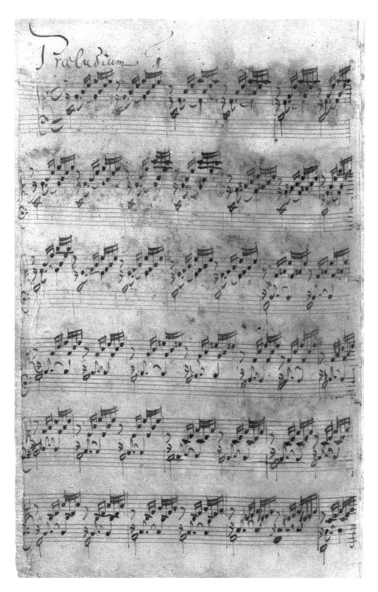

4. Johann Sebastian Back, Preludium in C from the first book of *Das Wohltemperierte Clavier*, autograph, Staatsbibliothek zu Berlin.

listen to it, preferably with the printed music to hand. Even if you can't read music, looking at the notes will still reveal plenty of information.

My advice to experienced students, though, is first to read, then to play, and then finally to listen to the performances of others. Why? Because by reading the notes, we come closest to the intentions of the composer. After this we have to form an image in sound, which is to say that anyone who can, should play the music themselves. Only then does it make sense to involve the performances of others. In our time, it is very easy and quick for most people to absorb music with so many audio examples within easy reach, but the risk is that we occupy ourselves more with the performance of the piece than the work itself.

When we want to play Bach's music, we are directly confronted with an important question. There are several versions of each piece, so which representation of the notes do we need? In many cases a manuscript has survived, but not always. Is it by the composer himself (we refer to this as an autograph manuscript) or by one of his students, a clerk or a friendly musician? There are of course printed editions, sometimes from the composer's own time, and there are the often large quantities of later editions, which may or may not have been modified, corrected, or be based on accurate research. The manuscript of the first book of *Das Wohltemperirte Clavier* can be found in the State Library in Berlin. In Bach's beautifully flowing hand, this in fact contains only the notes; that is, no dynamic marks, accents or additions to indicate tempo or phrasing. This alone creates enough problems to be solved before a performance can be contemplated.

First, we should ask ourselves on which instrument this music should be played. The title page of the manuscript provides no specification, so you might think that any keyboard instrument would be sufficient: the organ, the harpsichord, the piano, even the accordion. Bach himself probably wrote these pieces with his clavichord to hand. As well as some harpsichords, he had many clavichords at home. The clavichord is an instrument of limited size that has a remarkably soft sound, and on which it is even possible to create some vibrato through the direct contact of the finger via the hammer with the string. Like a keyboard with headphones nowadays, it is very well suited to the composing husband who seeks to make music without bothering others, and equally to studious children, such as Bach's, to practise without disturbing the whole family.

Even if Bach did compose most of his works at home on the clavichord, those written for the keyboard were in fact intended for performance on the harpsichord or organ. While the clavichord is played with little hammers, the harpsichord is a plucked instrument. Through an ingenious system activated by pressing the keys, the strings are plucked with quill plectrums, making a sound that can fill a significant space with ease. Because there is no direct finger contact (unlike with a guitar, where the fingertips touch the strings), one might think that little variation could be brought to the sound. Nevertheless, it is also possible to make phrases on the harpsichord, and notes can be bound to each other in partial or whole musical sentences, indicated in notation by phrasing marks which appear as curved lines over the notes.

Bach provided no phrasing marks in the *Prelude in C major*, however; he assumed that a good player of the instrument would know what to do. The absence of these marks was later seen by pianists as a disadvantage. This can be explained in part by the loss of connection with old harpsichord techniques since the end of the 18th century, and in part since pianists were in search of a high degree of lyrical expressiveness based on phrasing and dynamics, which were not to be found in Bach's notation. So, his scores were provided with the necessary symbols.

Carl Czerny extensively adapted Bach's preludes and fugues to the wishes of his time. For us, these are the markings of the first half of the 19th century, and not those of the first half of the 18th. To bypass this problem, it is advisable to return to the original notation and to look for an edition based on Bach's own handwriting. These are often described as 'Urtext editions', and contain a clear indication of the sources used.

Even so, none of the best modern editions can give an impression of the performance practice of the time, of the way this music was played in the first half of the 18th century. Do all of these sixteenth notes have to be played exactly and almost mechanically in the same way, or would Bach have preferred a more rhetorical, somewhat irregular performance? Was he in favour of an approach based on the Italian or the French style? For a long time, we have particularly appreciated the 'objectivity' of his music, its intellectual craftsmanship. Without ignoring this quality, nowadays we have a preference for a more expressive approach. When it comes to the *Prelude in C major*, the printed notation would appear to propose the first option. However, on the basis of Bach's own handwriting and in favour of the hidden melodic elements in this music, I would like to recommend a more linguistic, speech-like approach.

In a study of Bach's music, the professional musician will seek to place the printed edition and the manuscript next to each

5. Johann Sebastian Bach, *Preludium in C major* from the first book of *Das Wohltemperirte Clavier*, in an edition by Carl Czerny, with tempo indication (Allegro), phrasing marks, fingerings and dynamic markings.

other, in order to obtain a better feeling for what the composer committed to paper. In an age of music notation software, it is difficult to imagine how a composer's handwriting could reveal much about his intentions. Look again at the *Prelude in C major*, as written by Bach himself. The way in which the broken chords are notated might say something to us about the natural and flowing movement of the music. Or is that mere suggestion? Bach's notation nicely shows the upward movement of each broken chord, but the restful atmosphere of the handwriting is conspicuous, and not only in the calm motion of the bass notes.

However, there is nothing in the handwriting about the speed at which the notes should be played, nothing about the tempo that Bach had in mind: not Allegro (jolly and neat), nor Andante (at a walking pace), nor Largo (slow and sustained). Listen to the various performances one encounters on CD or on the Internet. Some pianists interpret the *Prelude in C major* as a prayer, others as fresh and playful. What should we use as a starting point? Bach had no metronome – those were only invented at the beginning of the 19th century. However, traditionally we have always had an excellent, albeit relative tempo indicator with us: our heart. Everything that beats faster than our heart rate is easily perceived as quick, and everything that beats at a slower rate as slow. The fact that Bach gave no indication could mean that he assumed that each musician would instinctively choose the right tempo: the 'tempo ordinario', an ordinary pace. Our heart rate has been a good and frequently used guide for establishing this over the centuries, but it is not absolute.

Supposing that we use our heart rate as a starting point for Bach's *Prelude in C major*, then another question remains: is the tempo in that case based on each beat of the four notated in a bar (and thus also on four sixteenth notes per beat, as in the upper stave in the right hand), or on the half beat (e.g. on each of the two bass notes, as in the first bar)? Bach himself writes a C on the stave, by which he indicates that there should be four beats in a bar and not two (in which case there would be a vertical line drawn through the C). The movement of the tempo therefore runs over four beat units per bar. Given that we have a resting heart rate of about 72 beats per minute, on average, then the pace of every beat in this prelude can be taken a little quicker than one per second, which flows nicely. Whether Bach would have agreed with this, we shall never know.

The intention of the considerations above is to show that even with a work such as this prelude by Bach, which seems to be so concise, transparent and clearly constructed, a great deal of work has to be done before we can permit ourselves to form a judgement on the piece itself. After all, is what we hear in the concert hall or on CD indeed what the composer had in mind? In fact, the only thing that we know for certain is what is represented in the handwriting of the composer, or in a printed edition that has personally been authorised by the composer. Sometimes there are letters and explanations from composers that can provide further information, but everything that is said by colleagues, friends, theoreticians and performing musicians about music that they haven't composed themselves is second-hand ambient noise.

The *Prelude in C major* consists of 36 bars, with two chords per bar, whereby each chord is broken into arpeggios and spread over two beats. If we play the chords directly after each other without the repeats, we end up with a series of 35 consecutive harmonies. If we were to play one chord every second we would be finished in 35 seconds, which is perhaps not very exciting, but is enlightening for harmonic analysis. Bach didn't choose this shortened route, of course. Music as an art deals with time, so we want to hear time flowing: the full 36 bars of four beats each, and the entire duration of the prelude of approximately two minutes. The music simply sounds better with the smooth movement of a half-beat pulse (two per bar) in the bass, followed by seven sixteenth notes above it, by which we can feel, in each individual note, the sands of time slipping through our fingers.

Now let's look at the music more closely, beginning with the first half of the prelude (see fig. 7). The first four bars belong

6. Johann Sebastian Bach, *Preludium in C* from the first book of *Das Wohltemperirte Clavier*, the 35 chords.

together. In a single movement, the two chords of the harmonious C major in the first bar make a full circle in order to return to C major via two dissonant chords (a D minor seventh with the seventh in the bass, followed by a G major seventh with the third in the bass). This is followed by seven connected bars, beginning with four bars which twice bring a progression of similar kinds of chords, namely two chords on the tones *A* and *D*, followed by two on *G* and *C*. This is called a sequence. Incidentally, the order of each pair is beautiful: from consonant to dissonant, and not, as one would expect, from dissonant resolving to consonant. The chords on *A* and *D* are repeated, but in a different inversion and both dissonant, and finally, with the bass descending stepwise from *G* to *D,* we arrive on the dominant note of *G*, the fifth in the key of C major. If we imagine this musical curve as a half-circle, then we have arrived at the top and can therefore start making our way back to the final tonic *C*.

On the basis of this brief example we can immediately see how clear and effective this music's construction is. More broadly, his prelude can also be seen to consist of an equally clear and effective harmonic development. The work begins in the first bar on the tonic *C* with the major triad on *C*: *C-E-G*. In bar 11 we have

7. Johann Sebastian Bach, *Preludium in C* from the first book of *Das Wohltemperirte Clavier*.

arrived at the dominant of C major, the major triad on the note *G*: *G-B-D*. From bars 12 to 19 we make our way back to C major, at which point Bach could have stopped. After all, we have arrived at the tonic; but that would be too simple, and musically too shallow. In the subsequent nine bars Bach therefore raises the harmonic tension, a tension that should irrevocably be released in a renewed conformation of the fundamental tone of *C* in bar 28. But no, instead of rewarding us with that *C,* Bach deviates to a harmony consisting of five different tones (*F sharp-A-C-E flat-G*), which sounds even more dissonant (listen to the notes *G* and *F sharp* against each other) than the dominant seventh chord of the previous bar (*G-B-D-F*, with *G* against *F*).

From this point, Bach uses no fewer than seven bars to pacify the harmony, finally to return to C major in bar 35. If we look only at the bass notes, we notice that from bar 24 Bach repeatedly writes the bass note *G* in the left hand, the dominant in the key of C major. For eight bars, all of the harmonic tension is built up from this one bass note. Such a persistent bass is known as a pedal point. For all of these eight bars, we are held in a state of limbo as to the resolution of these harmonies. After this Bach still doesn't conclude the piece, but uses three extra bars, now on the bass note *C* – that is, on the tonic itself – still sustaining dissonant harmonies like a kind of stay of execution, before the moment of actual relaxation is granted with the radiant C major triad of the final chord. The play on sixteenth notes is just one way of hearing the flow of time. Another is the way in which tension and relaxation are paced in the harmonies, and in particular, how that relaxation is delayed for extended periods.

With the *Prelude in C major* Bach has not only provided an example of a meaningful exercise in keyboard playing, nor merely an effective harmonic construction, and not even merely a way in which we can be made aware of the phenomenon of music as sound over time. No, this prelude (and no less the fugue which follows) can also be considered the be-all and end-all of contemporary developments in the fields of physics and mathematics on which all music is ultimately based.

Various scientists had thrown themselves into the theory of music in the late 16th and 17th centuries, on the one hand in relation to the universe and the Earth's place in it, and on the other hand in order to answer the question of how a sound or tone is created and moves through the air. In the century prior to Bach's, the most important examples of this search were: *Harmonices Mundi Libri V* (1619) by Johannes Kepler; *L'harmonie universelle* (1637) by Marin Mersenne; *Principes d'acoustique et de musique* (1701) by Joseph Sauveur; and *Musicalische Paradoxal-Discourse* (1707) by Andreas Werckmeister. Directly or indirectly, Bach must have been aware of these writings. In addition, he was thoroughly acquainted with Werckmeister's music theoretical thoughts on polyphony and harmony, including his *Harmonologia musica* (1702).

For Bach, the composer's profession consisted of more than the invention of agreeable and tasteful melodies and harmonies. Well into the 18th century, composing was a true science. Indeed, wasn't this what Haydn meant when he said of Mozart that he had 'die grösste Compositionswissenschaft'? A solid knowledge of mathematics and astronomy was indispensable if a composer wanted to master his craft properly. Since the days of Pythagoras, people had been convinced that the harmony of the spheres formed the basis of musical harmony here on Earth: just as the distance from the Earth to the known planets (including the Sun) could be expressed in simple numbers, so could the different lengths of the strings and their matching tones which

8. Nicolaus Copernicus, *De revolutionibus orbium coelestium*, 1543. With the Sun (*sol*) in the middle.

yield harmonious intervals (see box 1). However, somewhere in the fourth century AD, Ariadne's thread (to which Fischer was referring with the title *Ariadne musica neo-organoedum*) – the thread that had helped people to escape the labyrinth of ignorance – broke. It was only through Copernicus and then Kepler that this thread was picked up once again.

In the core of their writings, the scientists Copernicus and Kepler both referred to the ancient Greeks, whose theories had remained in vogue until the 4th century. Copernicus and Kepler opened the eyes of many. As is well known, they adjusted the old theories to the latest discoveries and insights, namely that the Earth is not the centre of the universe, but revolves around the Sun. The distance of the planets to the Sun and in elliptical orbits to each other can be mathematically and therefore numerically established, and in turn, the proportions that emerge form the basis of the universal nature of music, and equally of the most elementary rules for composing itself. Thus technique and materials, or the ways of composing and the material with which composing is done, are conversely also embedded within the laws of the universe.

> We can easily imitate the tests by which Pythagoras, in the sixth century BC, arrived at his findings about the close relationship between string lengths and harmonious intervals. When we stretch a string (of a violin, guitar or piano) between two hooks and pluck it, it vibrates in its entirety and we hear – assuming that we have tuned the string in C – the fundamental note C. If we fix the string exactly in the middle and strum one of the two halves then we again hear a C, but this time an octave higher. The relationship of the part that vibrates to that of the entire string is 1:2.
>
> Now we fix the string at 1/3. When we vibrate the largest part of the string we hear the fifth (so the G). The relationship of the vibrating part to the whole string is 2:3. Then we do the same at a quarter of the length, so on the half of the half. Now we hear the C another octave higher. This note is also a fourth higher than the aforementioned G.

We can fix the string at various points whereby the relationship of the length of part of the string to the entire string is different each time. The relationship 4:5 creates a major third (from *C* to *E*), and 5:6 is a minor third (from *C* to *E flat* in the minor scale). Thus it is the relationships between the string lengths that produce the various intervals, and relationships of the simplest numbers – 1:2, 2:3 and 3:4 – respectively create an octave, a fifth and a fourth.

1st octave							2nd octave							3rd octave							
C	D	E	F	G	A	B	C	D	E	F	G	A	B	C	D	E	F	G	A	B*	C
|							|							|		|		|			
octave -----------------							fifth -------							fourth ----		major third		minor third			
(C to C)							(C to G)							(G to C)		(C to E)		(E to G)			
length of the chord:																					
1							1/2							1/3		1/4		1/5	1/6	1/7	1/8
(NB: in reality the B should be a low B-flat)																					

How do we link this notion to the *Prelude in C major* from *Das Wohltemperirte Clavier*? The title of the entire volume refers to a specific manner of tuning, for which no uniform rules had existed until the 18th century. Numerous possibilities were known, whereby it was of particular importance to find a method for tuning major and minor thirds as purely as possible, since these contribute a great deal to the character of a key and play an important role in three and four-part chords.

In so-called meantone tuning, which is based on pure thirds, there is an audible difference between the note *D sharp* as a pure major third on *B* (*B-C sharp-D sharp*) and the note *E flat* as a pure minor third on *C* (*C–D–E flat*). This means that when you tune a harpsichord in meantone tuning, you always have to ask yourself what the 'black key' between the *D* and the *E* represents: a *D sharp* (a raised *D* with a sharp sign in front of it) or an *E flat* (a lowered *E*, given a flat sign). After all, when you tune the relevant string as a *D sharp* because you are starting a piece in B major (of which the first three notes are: *B–C sharp–D sharp*), and you then want to modulate (change from one key to another) through a few intermediate steps to C minor (with its first three notes: *C–D–E flat*), then the *E flat* will sound terribly out of tune, since the note is in fact still a *D sharp*.

Since the end of the 16th century, people had been eagerly searching for a solution to the problem of these kinds of differences; that is, for a more equal system of tuning in which, for instance, the *D sharp* and *E flat* would be brought closer to each other. In this way they arrived at well-tempered tuning systems; the emphasis being on the plural, since well into the 18th century several such tuning methods existed at the same time, each of which was able to solve a part of the problem (but not infrequently created a new problem instead). There was but one system of tuning that solved all of the problems: equal temperament. This system of tuning means, in fact, being somewhat out of tune across almost the entire range of intervals, since every fifth and every third has to be adjusted (tempered), and all minor seconds (so between *C* and *C sharp*, between *C sharp* and *D* etc.) have to be exactly the same as each other. This results in the fifth being a little too narrow, the major third noticeably too wide, but we appear to have become used to it after more than two hundred years. Either way, composers can now modulate as much as they like. The note *E flat* sounds the same as *D sharp*, *G sharp* the same as *A flat*, but as a result, the individual character of different keys plays virtually no role any more, and the only real distinction we have retained is between minor and major.

This, of course, was not what Bach wanted. He was in heart and soul a composer of polyphonic music, of the multi-layered play of lines. He was a master of counterpoint. For him, the character of the music had to speak via the characters of the chosen tonalities, and the horizontal lines composed on the basis of these – in fact, as had been the case for hundreds of years. It is not without reason that the title of the volume is 'the well-tempered clavier', and not 'the equal tempered clavier'. In this collection, he wanted not to test our modern equal-tempered tuning, but the tempered tuning suggestions of Andreas Werckmeister. This allows many keys to be used that would previously have sounded out of tune in their un-tempered state, while at the same time keeping the purity of the thirds as much as possible. So much for the clarification of the title.

> We can easily demonstrate the existence of overtones or harmonics with a little experiment at the piano. Press softly with a finger of your left hand, thus without making a sound with the instrument, the key of a low *C*, and hold this down during the entire exercise. The felt damper that belongs to that particular string will be released from the string by pressing the piano key, allowing it to vibrate freely. Then, with a finger of the right hand, play the *C* an octave higher than the key that is still pressed down. If the right hand key is released, the note carries on ringing. This sound cannot be coming from the string that has just been struck, because by removing the finger, the key came back up and the damper became pressed against the string once again. The higher *C* is therefore resonating in the lower *C* string, of which the key remains pressed down with the left hand. Now do the same with the *G* above the high *C* that was just played, and then the *C* above that, and then the *E* above that, and the *G*. Each time one of the notes is played and that particular key is released again, the tone will resonate in that freely vibrating low *C* string. Every one of the tones you have played (*C-G-C-E-G*) is therefore a hidden part of the low *C* string, and can freely vibrate within it. These are the natural overtones of that low string.

In Bach's time, however, scientific research into the modes of the major and minor third, harmonies and tuning, was no longer exclusively connected with astronomy and mathematics, but increasingly to the physical nature of sound, such as the vibrations of a string or the way in which sound was carried through the air. In short, it dealt with the science of acoustics as established by Marin Mersenne, Joseph Sauveur and others. In the treatise *L'harmonie universelle* (1637) Mersenne was one of the first systematically to explore the harmonic tones of a string, also known as overtones. When listening to a note, he noticed that other, higher notes sounded at the same time. This was sometimes a fifth or a third, depending on the instruments, the room, or of the other instruments playing simultaneously. He assumed that other tones were hidden within the sounding one, vibrating along with it (see box 2).

Mersenne had also noticed that the harmonic tones of a bell are not the same as those of an organ or a string instrument. Apparently various kinds of overtones could resonate, depending on the instrument. Theoretically he was unable to identify the reasons or causes for this, but more than half a century later, Joseph Sauveur was able to solve this in his best-known study, *Principe d'acoustique et de musique* (1701). Initially, Sauveur also took what he could perceive by ear as his starting point, namely that a string that vibrates can produce multiple overtones at the same time, suggesting that it can vibrate in multiple ways simultaneously, as long as the vibrations are in proportion to each other.

In this way, Sauveur arrived at a theory of harmonics, which is also closely connected to the material of the object that is vibrating. Around 1700 it became clear that a note, such as our *C* in the test in box 2, has other notes enclosed within it. Our example is based on a low *C* and then the *C* that sounds an octave higher, followed by the fifth *G* above that, and then directly above that the triad *C-E-G*. Now, just for fun, play the first two bars of Bach's *Prelude in C major* and what do we hear? Exactly this theory, written out in arpeggios.

The *Traité de l'harmonie déduite à ses principes naturels* (1722) by the composer and theoretician Jean-Philippe Rameau is also founded on this theory, and indeed was published in the same year as *Das Wohltemperirte Clavier* by Johann Sebastian Bach. Rameau's focus was entirely different, however, to that of Bach's most important reference, Andreas Werckmeister. Rameau built his theory from one single tone and its natural harmonics, thereby claiming that this system was in fact dictated by nature itself. As we have already explained, Bach preferred the polyphonic possibilities and qualities of each individual key, the theoretical basis of which was provided for him in Werckmeister's tempered tuning. Both starting points can, however, be traced in Bach's *Prelude in C major*.

Having arrived at this point, we have yet to finish with Bach's *Prelude in C major,* since, like so many compositions from the past, this work also has its history up to the present day. This has nothing to do with evolving performance practice or the question as to whether we can permit this work to be performed on a piano or an accordion. No, this is about the piece as an object on which others have gone to work in their turn. As Bach reworked his own compositions without much anguish, so have other composers embraced his *Prelude in C major*, both literally and figuratively. One did this by adding an extra part, another by taking inspiration from elements of the prelude.

An early variant of this kind of musical reference can be found, to a certain extent, in the accompaniment to Schubert's *Ave Maria* (D 839), or actually *Ellens dritter Gesang*. Here, dyads are laid down as broken chords over a regular bass pulse, just as Bach spread out his arpeggios as garlands over a bass note. Schubert's piano accompaniment, together with the softly undulating melodic lines, which are ornamented here and there, create a gently swaying music. We can find similar examples throughout the 19th century. A remarkable tribute to Bach can also be found in Chopin's *Preludes opus 28,* since the first prelude is also in the key of C major and, to a certain extent, follows the scheme of Bach's prelude.

In the middle of the 19th century Charles Gounod arranged Bach's *Prelude in C major* to create the *Méditation sur le 1er Prélude de Bach* (1853) for violin and piano or organ. This was less complicated than it might seem, which can be heard by playing the highest notes of the first bars by Bach: *E-F-F-E-A-D-G-C*. Gounod's famous melody is, as it were, up for grabs. A few years later he brought out the same work in a vocal version called *Ave Maria*, of which a large number of arrangements have been made. There is even a setting by Gounod himself for choir, solo violin, organ and orchestra on a text from Revelation 7:12: 'Benedictio et claritas et sapientia et gratiarum actio, honor et virtu et fortitudo Deo nostro,' which is to say: 'Benediction and glory, and wisdom, and thanksgiving, honour and power, and strength to our God.' In all of these versions, Gounod left Bach's original largely intact, but he did elongate it by as much as 38 bars. He did so by means that included repeating bars and softening transitions by inserting 'rustling' arpeggiated chords, in this way turning the prelude into a meditation, but of a sugary variety.

Towards the end of the 19th century another, less romantic view on Bach's work emerged. People thought his music should sound direct, motorised and somewhat abstract, rather than sentimental or in any way expressive. Around the time of the First World War, this vision would lead to a new objectivity both in the performance of music from before Haydn and Mozart's time, and in the composing of new music. The latter was of course intended to provide an antidote for the hyper-romantic works of the *fin de siècle*. For instance, in this light, we can view *Doctor Gradus ad Parnassum* from Debussy's *Children's Corner* as a reference to Bach, although the irony in this case is more directed towards what Debussy saw as the dull etudes of composers such as Clementi and Czerny.

I will end this short list of Bach curiosities with Arvo Pärt's *Credo* from 1968 (the year of the student riots in Paris and Berkeley). At that time, Pärt had not yet become the composer of inventive, strongly tonal and meditative pieces of music. The *Credo* simultaneously quotes Bach's *Prelude in C major* and the *Ave Maria* by Gounod. At the beginning of the work Pärt contrasts Gounod's sweetness with a huge choral eruption, as if one had landed in an unknown Passion by Bach, thence to settle on Bach's actual prelude, but not for long. The music is derailed via increasingly more powerful dissonances and in a section with extensive improvisations. In the conclusion both Bach and Gounod return, this time in a lushly harmonic arrangement for choir and orchestra. After this we can only go back to the simplicity of Bach himself, but Pärt withholds the C major of Bach's closing chord. Pärt's score was both political and religious, but that is another story...

This brings us to one final vision that we can draw from the *Prelude in C major*, namely the key of C major as a symbol, since this is not just any key. It is the key built on the bass note C, the basic tone used again and again by theoreticians in their research. The note C was seen in Bach's time, in the words of Werckmeister, as 'the root from which grows the entire tree with all its fruits'. It is the note on which the harmonic series was demonstrated, and on which the basic intervals of our harmonic system was established: the octave, fifth, fourth, and major and minor thirds. It is from the note C in the bass that the major triad C-E-G was laid out as the harmonious Trinity.

There are really only 35 bars which make up the *Prelude in C major* from Bach's *Das Wohltemperirte Clavier*, 35 bars which can be performed in many ways and on numerous instruments, even though Bach probably intended them for his own harpsichord and wrote them using his clavichord. These bars carry an entire world with them, a world that led to their creation, and a subsequent world in which these 35 bars became unavoidable. With everything that has been put forward here my goal has been to highlight just a single point: that no piece of music consists only of what we hear. Every work represents a universe of thoughts, theories, research, experiences, processes and much more that is and remains unsaid. Nevertheless, we must also be able to leave all of this aside, and be able to listen to Bach's unique music without restraint.

8. Music and communication

If we define music as a non-verbal means of communication, the implication is that something is being communicated. The question, of course, is what? Is it tones? Or meanings? Is it a story? Or an abstraction? Some of the earliest writings testify that music is capable of being communicated and that it can indeed release our emotions and make them comprehensible. Does this mean, however, that music expresses something in its own right, or that it is the composer who expresses something with his music? The oft-quoted statement by Igor Stravinsky – 'I consider that music is, by its very nature, essentially powerless to express anything at all' – seems to provide an answer, but the context in which this pronouncement was made shifts its emphasis somewhat. Stravinsky asked a journalist a question: 'Suppose you went out and narrowly escaped being run over by a trolley car. Would you have an emotion?' 'I should hope so, Mr. Stravinsky,' was the response. 'So should I. But if I went out and narrowly escaped being run over by a trolley car, I would not immediately rush out for some music paper and try to make something out of the emotion I had just felt.'

This is not to say that Stravinsky's music expresses nothing, but that the composer at his desk or piano is not bent on *trying* to express something. He builds a work of art, he creates forms, lines and colours: he organises a journey through time, and where necessary he also knows the psychological tricks of the trade. For Stravinsky, music stands *above* reality, *above* people. It cannot be put into words. We cannot translate it into common or garden emotions. What the composer expresses is at the most a reflection of his personality, the influence of the time and the society in which he lives and works. Stravinsky was very much convinced that a composition is a construction, and not a confessional based on personal emotions. In this regard, his statement also suited the attitude generally prevailing after the First World War: music as an antidote against the hyper-romanticism of the *fin de siècle*.

Stravinsky's vision of the profession is captured in the following observation: 'In France people talk about a "compositeur de musique", which is surely sufficient. In my passport I have deliberately put "inventor and composer of music" as my occupation. A composer is not only an architect but also an inventor, and he mustn't build houses in which he is not prepared to live.' This sounds a little like Edvard Grieg's credo from his final years: 'Artists such as Bach and Beethoven have erected churches and temples to great heights. I would prefer, as Ibsen put it, to build houses in which people feel happy and at home.' However, Grieg did seek to express specific things in his music, namely his affinity with Norwegian national character and culture. There is therefore a real difference between Stravinsky and Grieg: the former thinks of the building, the latter of the happiness of the people who have to live in that building. The former behaves like an architect, the latter like a welfare worker.

For Stravinsky, the communication of emotion and expression was indeed irrelevant. He was not interested in the effect of his music, but in the structure. His music is all about the Apollonian and not the Dionysian, even if we can certainly trace the latter in his early work. This reminds me of that excellent comment Richard Strauss made about Richard Wagner: 'The head which composed *Tristan and Isolde* must have been as cold as marble.' What Strauss meant was that, in order to be able to write such a large, dramatic and complex opera, one would have to be lord and master over one's thoughts as a designer, and by no means should one allow oneself to be carried away by the story or one's own emotions. If this were the case, the work would never go beyond a few nice moments of inspiration without form or structure.

To ensure that we listeners can be touched emotionally by music, the composer must be able to play us with his complete mastery of the trade, and with all his psychological insights. There is no room for personal emotions. Stravinsky therefore connects expressiveness and expressionism with individualism, and as its opposite, suggests the clear lines of cubism as an expression of personality. 'While individuality is suspect, personality never is, being almost a divine concept: the quality that you have as a gift from God.'

According to this way of thinking, Monteverdi, Purcell, Bach, Mozart, Beethoven, Chopin, Schumann or Wagner were not so much trying to express themselves in music, but more constructing, building, and putting music together. After all, to compose literally means putting together. The nature of the craft which composers undertake and their way of working is at the same time the imprint of their personality. But that labour and all that effort, which can take weeks, months or years, must be driven from somewhere and remain under pressure if the composer wants to reach the finishing line. The spark that sets the flywheel of composition into motion is the inspiration that makes you realise what you have to do as a composer.

If music as such expresses nothing, at least not in an active sense or from within itself; if it is not about the emotions of the composer, nor a reflection of his desire to define himself or to stand out (but at the very most a reflection of his personality and his craftsmanship); what then is the subject of a musical work? What is music about? Is it about the process of its own creation? About the relationship of the Earth to the planets? About a notion of divinity as a part of ritual and belief? About its own function and position in the community of people? Or is it only about the distance of notes from each other: the intervals, horizontal and vertical? About melody and harmony, and therefore only about itself? Is music a statement of itself or of the world that surrounds it? You could also ask: does it point inwards, or outwards?

There is no single answer for this. It is a matter of conviction, of vision. For Stravinsky music points inwards, it is about itself. He wouldn't have returned home to convert his emotions into music after nearly being run over by a trolleybus. Richard Strauss, on the other hand, translated his jaunty walk through the Bavarian Alps from Garmisch-Partenkirchen into a substantial orchestral work, *Eine Alpensinfonie*. Of course, he did so with a head of marble, as an architect of his music, but despite this cool mastery of his craft he emphatically wanted to tell his audience a story, to provide a musical experience as a parallel in sound to his walk. Claudio Monteverdi believed that the harmonies in music should follow and point out the words of a text. For him, music is a reflection of the words he has set. Hanns Eisler wrote many a work intended to send out a political message, such as the impressive cantata *Die Mutter*, and Bach saw his works as a representation of his piety, of divine laws. So, who is in possession of the truth?

Indeed, an answer to this is impossible to give. We can investigate what others have said on this subject over the centuries, and why. Or we can go to work empirically by listening to music and again and again asking ourselves what we hear, what is music's meaning or motive. Let's take once again the *Prelude in C major* by Bach. Through listening, can we create an image of certain extra-musical representations: a road, a walk, mountains or trees? Or do we only listen to tones and harmonies, and is every reflection on matters that occur beyond the music purely symbolic? Do we indeed see the planets rotating around the Sun, or do we count the number of chords and bars and take delight in the architecture of these few minutes of music?

While listening we can in fact determine little else than what we are trying to follow and what passes by our ears. There is rhythm and harmony, the passage of time, perhaps, but do these tell us anything other than what they themselves are: rhythm, harmony and time? Would Bach actually have been thinking of something else when composing these notes? About expressing his emotions? About the pursuit of pure beauty? Or did he think about nothing beyond the notes he wanted to write, and that he wrote at that moment? He might have been disturbed by his children playing or practising in the next room, or have had his mind on money still owed to him, or on lessons and rehearsals which needed organising: or are these things too mundane?

As listeners, we have no idea what thoughts were going through Bach's mind. We only have the notes as they have been handed down to us, set against the time in which they were composed – a time which has long since passed – set against the present, the time in which we are listening. While listening, the 'past' does not exist. All of the music that we hear in a concert hall, on the radio, via the Internet or in other ways, is current at the moment of listening. Only when we do not listen actively, and perhaps when we daydream or are distracted by thoughts beyond the music that we are hearing, can the past become a part of that which is heard.

Perhaps this was also true for Bach at the moment of composition, that he wrote his music only in the here and now. All of the technique, every rule and law, all of the dos and don'ts are stored in the memory and firmly anchored in the consciousness during work. Would Bach have thought at every note: what now? Which choices must I make? Which divine proportions shall I use here? Or could he trust his knowledge and ability to the extent that his only thought was: how do I write a piece for harpsichord in C major which goes from A to B, and is a good introduction for the fugue which is to follow? Compare this to a traversal of the city, during which we have no need for a constant re-discovery of every traffic regulation or each action while driving to be able to make the necessary choices.

Because the *Prelude in C major* is an abstract piece of music, a prelude and no more than that, we can easily accept an abstract approach. This music is not about David and Goliath, as is the case in one of the *Biblical Sonatas* by Johann Kuhnau, nor about the agony of Christ, as in Bach's *St Matthew Passion*. In addition, texts are sung in the *St Matthew Passion*; the story is told with both words and music. You would think that Bach must have introduced emotion into the work, and in fact today we consider this music to be remarkably emotional. People in the Leipzig of Bach's day were even concerned about the theatricality and 'un-churchly' nature of his music.

However, it is unlikely that the theatricality perceived by the Church Council in those days has anything to do with the emotions we now recognise in this music. Bach's theatricality was based on the rules of musical expression: how to imply grief, and how to suggest suffering. This applies equally to the rules governing the correct pose of a statue or a figure in a painting. Bach's *St Matthew Passion* is no Italian opera, but it does possess the forms so beloved of the genre: *secco* recitatives (with only the accompaniment of a harpsichord) and *da capo* arias (with their structure of having an A section, a B section, and then back to the beginning – hence the term *da capo* – for the repetition of the A section). The formality of the expression is not identical to the emotion of composing or even listening. Where the 18th-century listener might have been startled by the vehemence of Bach's means of expression, the 19th century the listener might have needed a handkerchief.

In Bach's time, the *St Matthew Passion* was one of the many passions which were newly composed each year for Good Friday, usually with a date stamp: best before… Now the *St Matthew Passion* has become a musical confession of faith of a higher order, timeless and sublime, concrete and abstract, pure sound and loaded with meaning, suitable for every moment of the year but most played on Palm Sunday or Good Friday. Bach's music is multi-layered. For some it points inward with its beautiful melodies, sometimes heartrendingly poignant harmonies, complex choral writing and detailed chorales. For others, the melodies and underlying harmonies are the essence of suffering, betrayal and humility, the choruses that of collective confession and aggressiveness, and the chorales filled with devotion. We believe that Bach specifically intended and wanted it this way.

Back to Stravinsky: might it be that what is valid for Bach's music is also the case with that of Stravinsky? That the listener can be allowed to interpret with absolute freedom and arbitrariness, regardless of the attitude of the composer? This is my preferred point of view. Once completed, the work of art becomes the plaything of every listener, and no less of each and every performing musician. Even composers who have written much about their music (such as Wagner or Mahler) or who during their lifetimes worked intensively with performing musicians (such as Ligeti and Stockhausen), cannot prevent their music becoming free as a bird after their deaths.

This, however, does not solve the question as to what music actually is about. At most, it addresses the problem of how we have approached it through the ages. So I ask once again: what is music about? According to the Viennese theoretician and critic Eduard Hanslick in *Das Musikalisch-Schöne*, music can express nothing other than musical ideas: themes, harmonies, rhythms, timbres. Music consists of 'tönend bewegte Formen', which can be translated as 'sounding shapes in movement' or 'sounding shapes over time'. This formalistic approach fits very well into a society and a culture in which the ethical function of music (by which is meant its intended usefulness) is not pivotal, but rather its beauty, its aesthetic function.

How many listeners do not enjoy Bach's *St Matthew Passion* without experiencing it as religious and liturgical, as a score that in essence was written for confession? For many, it is simply very beautiful music that you can also listen to in July or at the end of December. Thus we have formalised Bach's passion into an abstract piece of music. It has become an expression of beauty and not a work with any religious meaning. In fact, it no longer matters whether we talk about the *St Matthew Passion* or about Wagner's *Der Ring des Nibelungen*, or about the *Missa Papae Marcelli* by Palestrina or even the hymns in unison of the Church of Rome known as Gregorian chant or plainchant. For us these are either works of aesthetic enjoyment or not. Period. This is the way we listen to the music, connecting it exclusively to ourselves. We enjoy, we become emotional, we undergo a transcendental experience.

Is this what music is about – ourselves – individually and collectively? If this is true, then music is about everything we want to hear in it; we can connect it with any association that occurs to us. Even when music is provided with a text, as with an opera, oratorio, choral work or song, the strength of the melody, harmony and rhythm – what Hanslick called the basic elements – is apparently so great that they take a central position in our listening process. We do not recite texts as we leave the concert hall or opera house, but we do sing the melodies that have remained in our memory. Since this is the way we deal with music, we are very easily influenced by extra-musical suggestions; something against which even many a composer has been unable to protect himself.

9. Music as notation

Music has been made since time immemorial, and for the majority of its existence this music has been handed down orally. People listened to each other and sang or played based on what they had heard. Thus as listening and learning, music has been transferred from generation to generation for centuries. On occasion, musicians might have had support in the form of symbols that show whether the musical line rises or falls, or that uses a letter code for the tones, or through symbols that indicate fingerings for performance on an instrument. Long before the commencement of our calendar, the Chinese, Sumerians and Babylonians, Egyptians, Hebrews and ancient Greeks knew about these kinds of music notation.

Moreover, hieroglyphics show that the Egyptians also had a more physical and visual means of communicating symbols, whereby signals could be given with the arm, hand and fingers in gestures that must have been sufficient for singers to perform music together. Although this *cheironomy* is not written notation and the hieroglyphics serve as a report of a specific event rather than a score, these could serve as a musical record for us, given some knowledge of the meanings of the symbols (see fig. 9).

9. Two singers giving *cheironomic* directions and two wind players, tomb of Saqqara near Memphis, ca 2400 BC (photo © Effy Alexakis, Macquarie University Ancient Culture Research Center).

Each of these early notation techniques provide symbols (figures, letters or the depicted hand position) for the note which should be sung, the direction in which a melody should go, or which fingerings need to be used on an instrument, as for instance in notation for the Chinese zither, the *ch'in*. It was not until the 9th century AD that there was any substantial change in this, when the first methods were developed to preserve the music of the liturgical chants of the Church of Rome, of plainchant or Gregorian chant. These forms of notation, also called neumes, are in some ways comparable to the manner in which so-called *ekphonetic* notation was applied to Hebrew and Byzantine texts. Here, the shape of a musical phrase was indicated with a set of dots and dashes that floated freely above the text that was to be sung (see fig. 10).

Neumatic notation became increasingly complex, however. In the 11th century it therefore became necessary to introduce horizontal guiding or ledger lines above the text in order to define the pitches of the multitude of dots and lines more clearly. In around 1025 AD the Benedictine monk Guido of Arezzo gave musical notation an important impulse by proposing that one of these horizontal lines be marked as a line of coordination, for instance by adding the letter C in front of the line so that every tone which is notated on that line can be identified as the note C. From this principle emerged not only the C clef, but also the F and the G clefs. With these kinds of marking on staves of three, four and later five lines, music notation became so clear with regard to pitch that even less well-trained outsiders could gain an impression of the melodic shape of the chants.

From there, it was ultimately a small step to notate other facets of music. Within a few centuries, the notation of pitches evolved in Western culture from being little more than an indication and memory aid into an entirely independent reading text. At the same time a system of note durations was developed, through which rhythm and metre could also be written in a nuanced way. This had previously been limited to some set formulas, for instance by indicating above a piece of music that

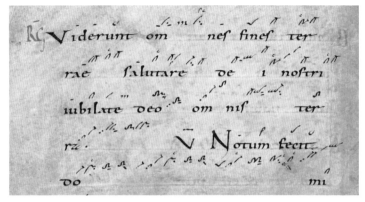

10. *Viderunt omnes, ekphonetische* notation, 10th century, Cod. Sang. 359, Stiftsbibliothek Sankt Gallen.

it should be read as a continuous sequence of note durations that are long-short or short-long, for example. Regardless of the text or the meaning of the words, everything was sung in the same rhythmic straitjacket.

The almost exclusive use of beating in groups of three in most early music was linked to the theological notion that the number three is connected to the Holy Trinity, and is therefore perfect. A three-part measure was considered a Tempus Perfectum: a consummate unit of time, represented by a closed circle. In comparison, the two or four-part measure is a Tempus Imperfectum: an imperfect unit of time indicated by a half circle. This sign is still our alternative notation for a 4/4 bar. On the basis of this vision, we can also find an explanation as to why a three-part time signature is used in many compositions at liturgically important moments.

With the development of mensural notation in the 14th and 15th centuries (the mensure indicates the duration of a note), the possibilities for melodic, rhythmic and metrical nuance were further extended, step for step, as required. The notes in a piece of music could therefore be brought closer to the essence of the text. Melodic lines could also be given ever greater flexibility and naturalness. Mensural notation finally became so refined that complex polyphony was possible. Even then, this music was not notated in the form of a score with all of the parts under each other, but in a choir book, often with the voices written entirely independently under each other and on the left and right pages (see fig. 3). These works must also have been composed in this way: voice after voice, presumably from memory, and in the fullest confidence in a theory of music that had been proven over many centuries.

It was only as late as the 16th century that possibilities were sought for developing notation in a score format. Both the complexity of the music of the time and the rise of notated independent instrumental music, such as the rhythmic and metrically simpler dance music, contributed to this. Since all of the voices in dance music move together rhythmically – the opposite of polyphony – it was easier to set the voices neatly under each other. Thus we can instantly see the simultaneity in the voices and imagine how they sound through reading. The notation of music as we generally still use it today arose in this way in around 1600.

In subsequent centuries this score system was refined still further, until in the course of the 20th century almost every musical thought, every nuance and every performance technique or way of producing sound could be written down in the smallest detail. This happened to the extent that performing musicians became entangled in a harness of instructions and commands, which led to a powerful urge to give performers more space for their own musical input by the second half of the 20th century. This resulted in extremely liberal graphic scores in which there is little more to be seen than a few lines, dashes and dots, sometimes even mere drawings which seem to have come from a comic book, or which in extremis go little further than a concept.

Nevertheless, notated music, such as that in a score, can never be a substitute for real sound. In the mind of the reader, any notation of music will always be supplemented with content that is personal and time-bound. Anyone performing notated music from the 10th, 16th or 19th century cannot avoid the performance being coloured by the fact that the performer is alive in the present, and that he is likely to have heard earlier performances by a musician who may have lived in 1970, and who, in his turn, will have been influenced in his interpretations by the state of knowledge and the vision on music of his own time and the times before him. We must also not forget that the listener, too, is alive in the present, and therefore gives substance to what he has heard from this perspective.

It is quite impossible to return to the time in which a certain piece of music was composed. Music's notation gives us too few clues to gain a real impression of the sound that may have been intended at that time. As well as this, our knowledge of music before 1900 is seriously impeded by the total lack of first-hand examples in sound. There are no recordings of Josquin, Bach or Mozart, or of Beethoven, Liszt or even Wagner, performing their own music. Only from the generation of Mahler and Debussy onwards do we have forms of sound reproduction, however elementary and imperfect these might be.

Even when we have examples in sound of Mahler, Strauss, Stravinsky, Hindemith, Schoenberg or Boulez, we still have to conclude that each of these masters has only been able to give a partial disclosure of his compositions, namely that part which the symbols of the notation were able to reveal at the moment of the recording. Quite often, at the time a particular composition was recorded, the composer had already moved on in the development of his music. Finally, the question remains as to whether the composer is the best performer of his own work. Might he perhaps be too fixed in the original idea of his work to be able to release it and allow it to have a new and independent existence?

There are enough surviving recordings by composers performing their own work that confirm that others can do this better, although the question then arises as to what 'better' means in this case. Set against the score as a compromise between dream and reality, there are no standards for a perfect performance. A nice anecdote might clarify this. One day Igor Stravinsky was rehearsing his ballet *Le sacre du printemps*, while the famous conductor Otto Klemperer sat in the hall following the music with the score on his lap. Both of these gentlemen were old and experienced, and Klemperer had conducted the *Sacre* himself many times. All of a sudden Klemperer closed the score with a bang and said clearly, 'The score is wrong.' The question is, how are we to interpret this remark? Did Stravinsky as a conducting composer go his own way, once again proving that a score is a mere compromise? Or was Stravinsky not a good enough conductor to do the score justice, and was Klemperer trying to avoid saying that in so many words?

In short, the notated score of a composition has only a symbolic bond with its creation, and from the moment that it is released into the world by the composer (in autograph, handwritten copy, in print or otherwise), it will lead a life entirely of its own. Through its notation, music has ceased to be an exclusively physical, concrete means of communication – the sound as it was imagined by the composer and realised by each performer – but has gained a material and abstract existence. It is indeed this communication on paper that has contributed to, and has even been the principal cause of the explosive development of Western music: the music for which such notation has been developed the furthest.

We are not only talking about the way in which the most complex polyphonic music has been created in Western culture, such as large-scale symphonic works, operas, string quartets, oratorios, masses and so much more. Interculturally and nationally, music notation has ensured that a multitude of folk and world music has been written down, and this has partially allowed it to be preserved in a fixed form. Even more than notation, however, modern sound recording technologies, from wax cylinder to digital media, have forced this music into a straitjacket of set sound and interpretation. Much has been preserved and made available to us as a result, but at the same time a part of the natural process of change, something so distinctive to a developing culture, has become almost impossible.

In saying this, I do not want to give the impression that everything is doom and gloom; quite the contrary. The possibilities have become limitless precisely because of the many ways in which music can be captured. Reading and playing, every musician makes his contribution to notated music. After all, unlike audio recordings, a composition inscribed in symbols leaves ample space for numerous individual additions and interpretations, whether or not they are trapped in the temporal framework of a recording.

10. Music as a temporal art

It is Wednesday evening, shortly before the start of the concert. The programme is that of a single, substantial work, Bruckner's unfinished *Ninth Symphony*, with his *Te Deum* as a fourth movement. Just after seven o'clock, the conductor is sitting in the green room. He prefers to prepare for a performance in peace. Right from the beginning, the first movement demands much of everyone's concentration and focus. It is an enormous task to make the 'Feierlich' and 'Misterioso' sound weighty but not dragging, profound but not tormented, devout but not pathetic, and certainly not sentimental. He feels the tension slowly growing inside himself.

An elderly gentleman arrives at the venue in a hurry, just minutes before the start of the concert. He has high expectations of this performance of *The Ninth*. Examples from the past with great names such as Eugen Jochum or Sergiu Celibidache, which were authoritative, fervent, and utterly solemn, are his ideal performances. Bruckner's music is like a prayer or a kind of sacrament for this man. The concert hall is his church and the conductor his priest. As he sits down he notices a well-known reviewer from the city newspaper positioned a few rows behind him.

One of the violinists on stage had worked on the symphony that morning. He thought it was a boring and mediocre rehearsal, with little more than a few adjustments to the balance. There was hardly a moment when they had been 'making music'. After the rehearsal he had to teach all afternoon at the music school, and then there was the rush home, a bite to eat, a quick change into concert clothes and on his bike through busy traffic to the concert. On top of that he is also in a bad mood from a quarrel at home that morning, and pupils getting under his skin during the afternoon. And now there is this long symphony of which he is already no great fan – with all that glutinous stuff and those excessive outbursts of sound.

At exactly a quarter past eight, everyone is in place. The orchestra has tuned, the musician contemplates the long musical journey ahead, and the reviewer has his pen at the ready. He knows the conductor and his performances, Bruckner's *Ninth* and the orchestra. The elderly listener is still puffing from all that rushing about. The conductor stands, deep in thought, behind the doors to the stage in the main concert hall. A porter opens the doors. The audience applauds. The conductor doesn't hesitate and swiftly descends the stairs; one must not be given the impression that he is an old man. Once on stage he winds his way between the orchestra chairs to the conductor's podium, bows, and raises his arms for the initial downbeat. After a few bars, he notices it: he has started faster than intended. That's what you get if you don't pause for a moment and take a deep breath.

The violinist in the orchestra, the reviewer and the listener are all surprised. The musician notices that the tempo is quicker than was agreed during the rehearsals, but is relieved that the performance will not be so painfully long, at least in this first movement. The reviewer, however, thinks the beginning is too fast, which he hadn't expected from this conductor. And the listener? He actually considers the opening to be curiously slow. He already finds it difficult to concentrate in his state of tension and breathlessness, and then to be confronted with such a slow beginning?

It is clear: none of these four people respond in the same way to the opening moments of Bruckner's *Ninth*. These are the same notes played in the same tempo, the tempo that the conductor has indicated and started. However, the effect of what is heard is dependent on numerous other factors. This means that what is heard is not the equivalent of what is perceived.

Hearing is to a great extent dependent on listening to what is sounding, and therefore on the listener himself; whether he is a conductor, playing an instrument or 'merely' part of the audience. For each of them, the click between the music and themselves depends as much on their own psyche as of that of the composer who has written that piece of music. On top of that, the non-performing listener in the hall is also dependent on the psyche of the performing musician. After all, the latter translates the composer's notes into a sonic experience for the listener. In the case of the aforementioned performance of Bruckner's music, three different perceptions of time and tempo play a role: that of the composer (as far as we know), that of the conductor with his orchestra, and that of each individual listener.

Each of these people experiences time in a different way. The tempo chosen by the conductor for Bruckner's 'Feierlich und misterioso' determines the experience of time for everyone involved. But this is not 'the' time or clock time, thus the actual duration of the music, but 'a' time, a 'virtual' time, an 'experienced' time. This 'virtual' time is the result of a combination of emotions and associations triggered in the listener by the music, both in his body (physical experience) and in his head (spiritual experience). To be more precise, it is in fact not the music itself that transmits its unique and exclusive emotions. It is inalienably our own emotions, individual to every listener, which are excited by the music, by the associations that the music evokes in us, and by the elements of tension and relaxation, speed, rhythm, dynamics, colour and sound that it contains.

The philosopher Susanne K. Langer pointed out in *Philosophy in a New Key* (1941) and *Feeling and Form: A Theory of Art* (1953), two studies that were controversial in their time, that it is the emotions generated by ourselves and not the emotions in the music as such that make us respond emotionally. This means that each listener bases his personal interpretation of the music he has heard on his own network of (private) emotions and (private) associations. Langer connected this to the notion that art as a language of symbols is 'analogous to our emotional life'. The emotions we derive from music are therefore in reality the consequence of parallelisms between the elements of music, and physiological and associative activities in our bodies.

The conductor, the musician in the orchestra, the reviewer and the elderly listener – each with their own associations, listening experiences, physical condition and psychological frameworks – had individual responses to the first minutes of that performance of Bruckner's last symphony. The conductor decided not to adjust the tempo as the music progressed. Thus the interplay of lines became easier to manipulate, the shapes sounded less forced, and the harmonies seemed to him less rough-hewn. He noticed anew that there is no such thing as 'the tempo' of a piece of music. Even the violinist in the orchestra let himself be carried away by the music. The reviewer noted that life was being blown into Bruckner's music, and that it seemed to take flight.

What about the elderly listener who was in such a hurry? His heart gradually relaxed and slowed. Was it the music that caused this, or his own ability to concentrate? Time seemed to float. The man became disconnected from clock time, and even from the chair on which he was sitting. He was all ears, and entirely immersed in the cosmos of Bruckner. Spirit and body became one. He could enjoy the music intensely as time-art now, and indeed even connect the smallest of nuances with each other through time. In the end, it was he himself who achieved this, but without Bruckner's music and the performance by conductor and orchestra, this would never have succeeded.

And all the while, someone was sitting next to him who was noticeably bored to death for the entire performance, caught up in what he felt as the 'doom of temporality'. Bruckner's notes flowed over him and he was incapable of holding onto them: they slid like water between his fingers. What was the reason for this failure in communication with this person? Let's assume for now that all art ultimately depends on the receptiveness of the beholder. To open up those shutters it takes more than the choice of a certain tempo, more than Bruckner's notes alone and more than the sounding of music in space and time. First of all, we need an ear that wants to listen, and which is capable of hearing. Without this, the music that sounds through the concert hall cannot become a newly created reality, nor an analogy for the emotional life of any listener.

11. Music and emotion

What is more self-evident than the relationship between music and emotion? Surely we need waste no more words on this? Music goes from heart to heart, and nothing can touch us more deeply. No other art form is capable of moving us so directly. According to some researchers, even the Neanderthals recognised a difference between the language of emotions (music) and the language of concrete messages (words). Nonetheless, 'music and emotion' is a fraught and complex subject for scientists. For many centuries we have wanted to know why it is that we respond so strongly to music, and researchers and theoreticians have tried to establish the connection between music and emotion in systematic terms.

No doubt it began with the simple observation that when music sounded, it was able to change the emotions of listeners. Are you in a bad mood? With a cheerful tune you will soon feel better. If you are in good spirits and you listen to a melancholy composition then your frame of mind can be overturned. It is as if we respond to music like a thermometer. We feel every nuance and each change of temperature without having studied the piece, without any need for knowledge about or understanding of music. For many people, this is the mystery of music.

On the basis of similar experiences, Kant concluded that music could not be grasped cognitively, that it could convey no image of concrete reality and that its function was more for pleasure than as a part of culture. For this reason he positioned music at the bottom of the scale in relation to other forms of fine art, since it only works on our feelings. Kant was of the opinion that music has no effective aims, and exists only because of its beauty. Music serves no purpose, but is sublime: it stimulates the world of our ideas, by which is meant Platonic ideas. Thus we can project our image of beauty onto music, and that is its purpose.

The point is not whether music should for this reason be at the bottom or the top of the scale when it comes to the fine arts, nor whether we agree or disagree with Kant that music cannot be grasped cognitively. In my opinion, Kant's remarks just show that he had no affinity with the profession, and understood nothing of the inner laws and rules of music. Joseph Haydn showed a diametrically opposite vision when he complimented Leopold Mozart on his son, admiring his great knowledge with regard to composing ('die grösste Compositionswissenschaft') and his good taste. Both observations were important arguments for Haydn when considering his young colleague as being one of the greats. There was no mention of the most beautiful or the most moving music. Emotions of that sort played no part in Haydn's judgment.

They did for Kant, however, and this is why he gave music a separate status that is largely a result of its inexpressible and elusive qualities, and the immediacy of the emotions that are triggered in those who listen. In this way, Kant artfully manoeuvres music from the mind to the heart, from mathematics to the psychology of mystery, from skill and craftsmanship to the disembodied feeling of pure inspiration, from science to pleasure. The consequences this had for the development of music in general and for the place it has since been given in society is the subject of a different story. The fact that music seems to have no other purpose than to display its own beauty and to feed our sense of enjoyment can be seen as a demotion, in terms of its status, but also as a promotion.

The question remains: does music itself contain emotions, or do we need to seek these in the listener? How do these emotions then occur? Can we label them? On which basis are we so sure that music contains emotions that can hit us at the most expected and unexpected moments? If we consider that a piece of music indeed contains a specific and definable emotion, then shouldn't every listener recognise and feel that specific emotion? If this is the case, then every listener should respond in exactly the same way to the first movement of the *Moonlight Sonata* by Beethoven or the ending of Tchaikovsky's *Pathétique*. Yet we know from personal experience how widely reactions can differ, even between like-minded people.

How often does it happen that two people are listening to the same piece of music, performed by the same musicians, in the same hall and under the same acoustic conditions, and that one is moved to tears while the other is truly bored? This is only possible when the emotions each person has are 100% his own, and do not come from the piece of music to which they are listening. Does the music therefore play no role in this? Of course it does, but not in the sense that the emotions from the piece of music are transplanted into the mind of the listener. What music delivers is a release of emotions in the listener: emotions that are not necessarily of the same class as one might recognise in that particular piece of music.

In a certain way, this is comparable with the way in which a sound arrives at the eardrum, but does not enter the brain. To enter the brain, it must be transformed into electrical pulses. The sound of music and the emotion of music remain divided between the outside and inside of one's body. The first is modulated from a wave into a pulse. The second undergoes not even that, but does result in an emotional experience, because an emotion in a piece of music can exhibit a parallel with the emotion of the listener. To paraphrase the words of the philosopher Susan K. Langer, through such a parallelism it seems as if the music passes on emotions, while in fact it releases emotions in us that are entirely ours. That is what music can do: unleash emotions in ourselves, our own emotions.

The result of this is that when listening to the same music, one listener may respond emotionally and the other not. This has nothing to do with taste, but everything to do with psychology, with our character, with our experiences and associations and any number of highly personal factors. It may be difficult to have differences of opinion with regard to taste, but in fact it is many times harder to expose your own mind to yourself in order to explain your personal reaction to music; as a listener on Freud's couch.

As students, we were shown the way into this uncomfortable terrain as the result of a provocative study by Leonard B. Meijer, *Emotion and Meaning in Music*. One day, the teacher of music psychology at the University of California in Los Angeles asked us to close the curtains, turn off the lights, and listen to some pieces of music in the dark. With this we were given some simple questions: whether we could hear if a piece of music was the first, second or third movement of a composition; whether we could determine if it was an abstract piece of music, for instance a movement from a symphony or sonata, or if it was a programmatic work, which is to say that the composer was consciously trying to tell a story in his work (*The Moldau* by Smetana or *Don Juan* by Richard Strauss); and finally, whether we could tell if the music changed something in us, and if so, what and how?

The teacher then played us an overture to an opera by Lully, the first part of Haydn's *Die Schöpfung*, the coda of the first movement of Beethoven's *Ninth Symphony* and some film music by Korngold (as far as I can remember it was from *The Seahawk*). What did we have to look out for? Actually, for an entire arsenal of details, such as the sound of a piece, the tempo of the music, the way in which the material was arranged or processed, the harmonic development and the use of the instruments. Our teacher considered our initial and unprepared responses equally important. What is your instant reaction, without any reflection or seeking to understand? The results were surprising to us at the time.

We found that many of our primary, impulsive reactions were based on the tempo and the direction of the music. The first of these is simple. A piece is slow or fast, it accelerates or slows down, although what is fast or slow: the beat or the development of the material, such as the succession of distinct chords? The second is more difficult to establish. How can you hear the direction of a composition? Techniques such as the thickening or thinning of the various intertwining voices can help, or the ways in which harmonies lead to other harmonies, or melodies are shaped. With more experience in listening it is possible to observe many details and nuances almost in passing, and with a little practice the brain often does this automatically. Music psychology is based on this automatic listening.

So we react almost as a matter of course to sudden changes in music, the fading of harmonic colours, unprepared dynamic transitions (a sudden loud sound in a quiet piece), changes in tempo or differences in rhythm. Each of these changes secures changes in the listener, too. There are entire handbooks with descriptions as to which effects lead to which reactions. This is valuable information for composers of film and advertisement music, but also for elevator music or background music at the dentist or in amusement parks; and there is no way we can avoid these types of music.

Even when we respond to music without thinking or impulsively, this is still almost inevitably the result of conditioning. From birth we are confronted by and surrounded with an endless amount of sound and music, and this applies not only to the present day, now that we can acquire and hear music with nonchalant ease almost all over the world. We store all of this music in our memory, together with the most important experiences encountered while listening, experiences which are sometimes connected to the music or which have nothing to do with it but remain associated thereafter. A fearful, sad or happy moment can forever colour the music we were hearing at that particular time.

For example, one day when I was a teenager, I was given a gramophone record from the former Soviet Union with Sergei Rachmaninoff's *Third Piano Concerto*. The pianist was barely older than me, something that already made a big impression. In addition the music was new to me. I knew the *Second Piano Concerto*, but not the *Third*. What was remarkable was that when I put on the record and the first bars from the piano came through the speakers, it began to snow (it was the end of December). This combination of Rachmaninoff's concerto with the snow outside has proved inescapable for me ever since. Even when hearing this music during a heatwave in August in France, in my mind it is snowing. This anecdote also says something about the way in which memory works: associatively, and on many, sometimes labyrinthine, levels. This can work in both directions: from the music to us, or from us towards the music.

We have all undoubtedly had experiences similar to mine with Rachmaninoff's concerto, such as with the music you might have heard during the funeral of a family member, or at the first meeting with a beloved. Smells, colours and sounds attach themselves easily to events. Numerous associations with moments from our life or our dreams, from books we have read or films we have seen, moments at which music played a conscious or unconscious role, ensure that the meaning a piece of music has for us can be many times more complex than the information distilled from a simple theoretical analysis. We are the emotion, and the music releases this in us. This is another reason we cannot do without music.

The following two anecdotes show us that these emotions are ours, and not those of the composer or the performing musician. The first is historical. In the 1930s, the famous violinist Bronislav Huberman performed a recital in the small hall of the Concertgebouw in Amsterdam. The programme contained one of the works to which he owed his fame as an artist, the renowned *Chaconne* from the *Second Partita* by Bach. Just before going on stage, his agent, Dr. Geza de Koos, told him that there were 423 people in the audience. Huberman's playing was heavenly, and the audience was moved to tears. After lengthy applause Huberman returned from the stage and said to his manager: 'Sorry, Geza, there are 431 people in the hall.'

By the same token, I remember a Dutch comedian who played the slow first movement of Beethoven's *Moonlight Sonata* at the piano, deep in thought. Suddenly he started to talk through this, revealing to the audience everything that was going through his mind: did I turn out the light at home, that train was really packed, I wonder why the children were fighting again this morning, it's the wife's birthday tomorrow... What we hear and the way in which a musician presents a piece of music doesn't have to be consistent with his thoughts or those of the listener.

A pianist can put his entire emotional life into that first movement of the *Moonlight Sonata*, say everything with those notes that he intended to say, and even then the audience might respond frostily and remain unaffected. The reverse can also be true. We can never be 100% sure that a pianist is sincere in his playing and his performance, in the same way as he can never be sure that the audience is sincere when they stand as one to give him his ovation. Is that applause really for him? Or is it a necessary act of liberation from the public? Or merely the shortest way to the bar or the cloakroom? Music and emotion: this remains a complex relationship, but we enjoy it intensely if and when it succeeds.

12. On depth and elevation

One day a student asked me if I could tell him something about the term 'depth' in music. Everyone talks about it, and most people more or less understand what you mean, but can you define 'depth'? That sort of question can put you on the spot as a teacher. Can we describe such a concept? Do we actually know what depth is? Depth in music: how often does a pupil hear, 'You play the music with technical proficiency, but it lacks depth'? Or, 'Can you give more depth to Beethoven's notes? At the moment the music is too superficial.' The latter remark should provide some clarity. Apparently, depth is the opposite of superficiality. But how deep is deep? Is there some means of measurement? The depth of a boat is at least measurable and is therefore concrete, but that of music?

The expression 'without depth' is often used as an alternative for 'superficial', bringing 'depth' into association with the word 'profound'. This is something about which you have to think a great deal, in which you need to immerse yourself in order to gain understanding. A person's profundity means that his thoughts are deep or many-layered, but in fact this is rather a relative term: many-layered in relation to what and whom? To other people or to yourself? We lack absolute terms for this.

A person who is used to thinking deeply about things and is intensively occupied with complex musical expression, might claim that a *Nocturne* by Chopin has little depth (by comparison with Beethoven's late string quartets, for instance), but that a performance of that *Nocturne* by Maurizio Pollini at least raises the piece above itself (which is to say, exceeds the expectations of that particular listener). Anyone who is unquestioningly bowled over by Chopin's *Nocturnes* can be disappointed by a performance that doesn't meet the ideal image that they have of both the music and its many possibilities in terms of performance. Judgements about 'depth' can therefore only be made in a relative sense.

If someone perceives a lack of depth during a performance of Chopin's music by Alfred Brendel, Maurizio Pollini or Lang Lang, then this says more about the listener than about Brendel, Pollini or Lang Lang. It doesn't mean that these virtuosos were having a bad day or were lacking in concentration. This is a possibility, of course, but even then, there is no direct connection between the degree of concentration or the nature or the mood of a musician and our reaction as listeners to their performance. If the 'click' between the musician on stage and the listener in the hall doesn't take place, the musician is not automatically the guilty party. The listener can also suffer from a lack of concentration or be feeling out of sorts. If a thousand people in a venue consider that a concert was not a success then the musician on his own can have little objection. However, this is not to say that the concert went badly; at most it indicates that the desired communication with that specific audience failed.

A term such as depth is actually nowhere to be found in philosophy, but references to its results are familiar. When a work of art, a train of thought or a musical performance is experienced as 'deep', the recipient is often described has having an 'exalted' feeling, carried away by something unimagined or which had not previously been thought. Something that is exalted, sublime or 'erhaben', as a philosopher such as Kant might put it, is that which rises above the purposefulness of the laws of nature. According to Kant, literature and the visual arts are incapable of this. He rates them highly, however, as they appeal to the intelligence, something which in his opinion is beyond the power of music. From this, however, it turns out that music is the art form *par excellence* that can be 'exalted', free as it is from everyday experience and the concrete world of things.

The experience of exaltation works even more strongly when the work of art leads to a feeling of sublimation, for instance when a composer or a performing musician removes all of the mundaneness from the music by an extreme magnification of the various elements from which it is made. This might appear to be a complex issue, but it is in fact easy to achieve. Listen to Erik Satie's first *Gymnopédie* in its recording by Aldo Ciccolini, and then to that by Reinbert de Leeuw. What the latter does is to sublimate the music by taking the tempo so slowly that this little piano piece becomes remarkable as a matter of course. Many might instantly seek to use the terms 'profound' or 'religious', but is this depth, or just a trick?

There are numerous ways to make something more remarkable. Every element of a composition can be used for this purpose: the tempo, the phrasing, the dynamics and so on. We can also find this phenomenon in the visual arts. Enlarging a small spider into a giant one, as done by Louise Bourgeois, or the distortion or transplanting of familiar forms or images, as can be seen in the work of cubists or surrealists, are all ways of realising increased momentousness through sublimation. Even the extraordinary proportions of Michelangelo's *David* in Florence, or a Gothic Cathedral somewhere in France, or so-called skyscrapers, buildings which seek to touch the heavens: these are all expressions of a desire for sublimation. And what are we to think of some of the extremely slow movements in Beethoven's piano sonatas and string quartets?

In 1739, the German musician Johann Adolf Scheibe wrote in *Der critische Musicus*: 'A true art may seek the natural, but only great art will also transcend this. This brings us into that which is contrived and nebulous. [...] Art must imitate nature. Once this imitation goes beyond nature then it becomes objectionable and turns itself against nature.' Scheibe is referring to the music of Bach, among others. Music that transcends everything, with the result that it is often unnatural. Is this a fear of the irrational, as we later encounter with Kant, or is Scheibe warning us about something we have often had problems with in the 20th century: the desire to sublimate and elevate everything, to make everything remarkable? Letting go of the rules of nature, those rules that have been considered the basis of all music for centuries, instils as much fear of as it does curiosity in that which is sublime.

'Great art' is in and of itself not objectionable. In Scheibe's vision, a composer has to be fiery and inventive to produce 'an exalted symphony'. He also has to put a lot of variety into his music: 'The one unforeseen variation must follow the other', and 'unexpected occurrences must similarly act in a surprising way to the listener'. The aim is therefore not to be found in the natural, but in the unnatural. In that case music cannot be seen as a logical reflection of the mind, which pursues naturalness; on the contrary, since music affects and alters the mind. Kant therefore also concludes that exalted art, or everything that we consider exalted, cannot be found in nature, since nature is purposeful and can therefore be regarded as an object of beauty, but not as something sublime.

According to Kant, exaltedness disengages itself from any concrete purpose. 'To be exalted is to make everything else seem small by comparison,' he wrote in his *Kritik der Urteilskraft* of 1790. We don't find exaltedness in nature, but only in our world of ideas, and there, in our world of ideas, is where music is created. In 1774 Johann Georg Sulzer wrote a contribution on 'Erhaben' in the *Allgemeine Theorie der Schöne Künste*. In this he came to the following remarkable conclusion: 'When order arises from chaos and confusion, it is an elevated thought for those who can see in some way the rightness of this, that from all of the apparent chaos in the physical and ethical world, the purest organisation can be realised.' In musical terms, this transition from disorder to order is beautifully exemplified in *Die Vorstellung des Chaos*, the first movement of Haydn's *Schöpfung*.

For E.T.A Hoffmann, however, it was Beethoven rather than Haydn who was the composer of sublimated and therefore exalted music. 'Beethoven's instrumental music opens for us the realm of the gigantic and the immeasurable. Luminous rays shoot through the night of this realm. [...] Beethoven's music cranks up the shuddering, the fear, the bewilderment and the grief.' Now that's what I call sublimation. Beethoven was the first known composer who saw it as an obligation and a duty to humanity and to himself to create music. For him, elevation was not exclusively an abstract concept derived from the writings of Schiller, no doubt including his *Vom Erhabenen*.

By composing exalted music, Beethoven in the first place pursued relief from his own suffering as a result of the deafness of which he was so ashamed. However, he was equally convinced that this would also help others. Exaltedness therefore became a highly personal aim. His passion, his constructive capabilities, his great ideals and his individualistic and humanistic world view were the result of his own ambitions, his own enthusiasm and his talent, which in his opinion was God-given. In this he distinguished himself from the noble gentlemen on whose support he depended almost his entire life. They had their place in society thanks to the generations before them. Beethoven reached his position by working hard and by not wasting his talent. He elevated himself.

The image of sublimity around Beethoven's music has been given an extra impulse through his late string quartets. Never before had a composer intertwined the four voices of a quartet with each other so organically. A professional ensemble was indispensable for performances of these quartets, with their difficult performance techniques (high positions, great leaps and numerous rhythmic complexities). Mozart played his quartets mainly with friends at home in his living room. String quartets by Joseph Haydn, Louis Spohr and later those of Felix Mendelssohn could also be rehearsed by reasonably skilled amateurs for performance in domestic or courtly circles. However, from the outset Beethoven's were a risky undertaking, and even his first quartets are much more complicated than almost all of those by Haydn or Mozart.

Fortunately, Beethoven had one of the few professional quartets of his time at his disposal; that of Ignaz Schuppanzigh, also known as the Razumovsky Quartet, since the musicians were in the service of Count Razumovsky, the Russian envoy in Vienna. Schuppanzigh and his colleagues gave the first performances of most of Beethoven's quartets. After the death of the quartet's leader in 1830, three years after Beethoven's, it would take until after 1860 before other professional musicians dared to form a permanent string quartet and to perform Beethoven's masterpieces. The best known quartet at this time was Joseph Hellmesberger's. It was only after 1870, however, that the string quartet of Joseph Joachim, one of Johannes Brahms's best friends, laid the basis of modern quartet playing.

During the course of these decades, however, a change in mentality on the part of the public manifested itself. No matter how incomprehensible this may seem to us, Beethoven's late string quartets experienced considerable success at their first performances amongst the elitist, educated, aristocratic and *grand bourgeois* audiences of the time that came to the spacious salons of the city nobility to hear the newest works of the Viennese master. We can see this success reflected in contemporary reviews.

In an article in the *Berliner allgemeine musikalische Zeitung* in 1825, the well-known poet and music critic Ludwig Rellstab asked himself how someone would feel when in close proximity to a genius who had in life already acquired an aura of immortality, and to experience the premiere of a new work by this genius. He had recently heard three of Beethoven's late string quartets for the first time in performances by Ignaz Schuppanzigh's quartet. This concert took place in an environment with like-minded people. The atmosphere was solemn, subdued and focused. One of the composer's brothers was present amongst other close family members, all of them visibly very proud.

Barely a generation later, in around 1840, the balance of this audience had completely changed. Greatly impoverished by the Napoleonic wars, much of the aristocracy was noticeably less well educated, certainly when it came to music. In addition the tastes of the urban classes were different. People wanted lyrical melodies and folksongs; they looked for narrative elements in their music, for fairy-tales. With the exception of a few works, the music of Haydn, Mozart and Beethoven was considered to be too abstract and difficult to understand. New audiences looked for more drama, and chose the novelistic musical art of Carl Maria von Weber, Louis Spohr and Robert Schumann over the tragic power of Beethoven.

People no longer really knew how to approach Beethoven's late string quartets, with all those wide-ranging and entangled lines, which were hardly the kind of thing you could sing along with. No, such music was too complex and exalted for daily use, and demanded special training for its appreciation. That was music for the future, and a distant future at that. Anyway, many thought, Beethoven had been stone deaf when he wrote those quartets. Did he actually realise what he had composed? Only a handful of colleagues understood what a Titanic effort he had made. They saw that he had transformed the string quartet from something of a high-class social activity into a form capable of carrying a composer's most personal and individual expression.

Because of his reverence for Beethoven, Schubert at times was quite fearful of writing for this setting. After 1850, hardly anyone composed string quartets in sets of six as Haydn had done. In general, composing for string quartet had become a deadly serious, for some even a burdensome occupation. You could only penetrate this genre if you were able to turn strict self-analysis into pure art for art's sake. Thus the composer entered the darkest caverns of the soul and the seat of the unchanging will, to use the words of the philosopher Arthur Schopenhauer. Following in the footsteps of Kant, this important younger contemporary of Beethoven was of the opinion that all of the fine arts belong in Plato's world of ideas, with the exception of music, since this has no relationship with the concrete realities of the outside world. Music penetrates directly into and also emerges from the immutable will of life, the subconscious force driving all human actions.

Hence music was entirely removed from the realms of the intellect. There was no way of talking about music rationally, and even less so, about musical taste, since from this point of view these aspects are entirely individualistic. Composing in the 19th century therefore became a highly personal matter: an extension of the deepest of the most personal feelings. As the Dutch poet Willem

Kloos remarked on art in general: it is 'the most individual expression of the most individual emotion'. From this idea it was a matter of course that composers would increasingly want to profile, crystallise, polish and sublimate that most personal of facets of their creativity. And thus Beethoven acquired a symbolic status with exactly that aspect of his art. He had shown the way towards sublimation as the result of extreme individuality.

Whoever wanted to compose after him could, of course, decide to follow the path on which Beethoven had embarked and bare their soul in their music; just like Brahms, who only wrote three string quartets and even then with fear in his heart of the giant shadow cast by Beethoven. The same is to a certain extent true of Schoenberg and Bartók. The string quartet had become the domain of sublimated music, and at the same time it was for many a composer exceptionally suitable for the most intimate musical outpourings. Via the string quartet, the composer could forge a special bond with his listeners. And these soon perceived what was being presented to them in this genre: a transcendental experience, and a glimpse into the innermost being of the composer as well as that of themselves as listeners.

Such an experience is not based on the absolute laws of the cosmos, nor is it the result of a total mastery of the craft. No, for many listeners this comes from the highly personal relationship between the soul of the composer and their own soul, even when the composer was entirely unaware of this or had never pursued such a purpose when composing. In the 19th century the judgement of the witness as consumer became more important than that of the composer as producer. Bearing Kant and Schopenhauer in mind, good and important music had to be transcendental. It is this subjective transcendence which has defined many music lovers' relationship with music ever since. To end with a quote from the Dutch composer Matthijs Vermeulen from 1919: 'Music is knowing, music is belief. Music is the only reliable, public faith. Music is the eternal definitive certainty.'

Part C

13.   Beethoven: the Fifth

Long ago I was sent a cassette tape from a friend in the States containing a report on Beethoven's *Fifth Symphony* by the musicologist and musical comedian Professor Peter Schickele, alias P.D.Q. Bach. Yes, indeed: a report. Not an analysis, nor a musicological discourse but a report, straight from the field; and not the battlefield, as for instance in Beethoven's *Wellingtons Sieg, oder Die Schlacht bei Vittoria*, but a football field. From the starting gun, which commences even before Beethoven's ta-ta-ta-daa has sounded, to the cheers at the end, Schickele manages to clarify the general structure of Beethoven's music to every football fan and many others without using technical terms.

> And they're off with a four-note theme. This is very exciting; the beginning of a symphony is always very exciting folks. I don't know whether it's slow or fast yet because they keep stopping. It doesn't seem to be able to get off the ground yet… and it looks like, yes it looks like we're coming up to a cadence here folks… Ah, the violins didn't cut off there, a little trouble with the violins, they weren't watching. And there's that four note theme again folks, and another stop – just can't seem to get this piece off the ground…

If we look at the beginning of the symphony, this is indeed what happens in the music. 'Tell me Bob,' asks the reporter, 'do you think you'd call that four-note idea a theme or a motif?' Bob: 'Well, Pete, the technical term would be motif, which he uses to build a theme.' What Schickele does is ingenious. Without falling into the secret language that often envelops music and obscures things for so many devotees, he not only shows how the construction of this first movement of Beethoven's symphony unfolds, but turns the explanation itself into a thrilling experience.

It is also nice to discover that, despite the opening movement's C minor key and 'ta-ta-ta-daa', which has almost become a symbol for fate, fate here is actually in no way 'knocking on the door.' Fate in the *Fifth Symphony* is in truth no more than an invention of Beethoven's loyal associate and biographer Anton Schindler, who was quite unreliable when it came to facts. Schindler seemed to recall that Beethoven had once told him about this, but if that was really the case, then it is strange that there is no other source for this not unimportant detail. There is not a single statement on the subject by any contemporary, other than in one of Beethoven's conversation books, of which there are doubts about what Beethoven himself might have said. In fact, Beethoven's young pupil Carl Czerny had an entirely different memory, namely that Beethoven had heard this theme from the throat of a yellowhammer during his walks in the Prater.

The short-short-short-long motif, with the three short notes played lightly and with an accent on the long 'daa', is actually not that uncommon. Beethoven had already used it himself in the

11. Ludwig van Beethoven, first bars of the *Fifth Symphony*, autograph, Staatsbibliothek zu Berlin.

Fourth Piano Concerto and the *Piano Sonata in F minor*, known as the *Appassionata*. We also regularly encounter this motif in music from the last quarter of the 18th century, and not only in French revolutionary songs such as the *Marseillaise,* which begins with a variant on this rhythm. The *Marseillaise* leads us to Mozart' s *Piano Concerto in C major* (KV 503), in which the first movement is not only driven by the same ta-ta-ta-daa, but of which the central theme very much resembles the *Marseillaise*. The subsequent influence of Mozart on Beethoven is in itself not so exceptional, but is quite remarkable in the *Fifth Symphony,* since for many this symphony is a standard-bearer for romantic, emotionally charged and violently contrasting music. Nevertheless, the theme of the Scherzo in the *Fifth* reminds us of the finale of Mozart's *Symphony in G minor* (KV 550), and the second theme of the finale has a clear affinity with the melody from the slow movement of his *Symphony in C major*, the *Jupiter* (KV 551). This is no coincidence: Beethoven copied parts of these works by Mozart into the same sketchbook in which he scrawled the first sketches for the *Fifth*.

The entire symphony is all about war and freedom, and more generally about the positive promises that inspired citizens in big cities after 1789. Everything would finally improve: long live the free man! This sentiment is also reflected in works such as the *Hymne à la Liberté* (1793), the *Hymne à la Nature* (1793) and the *Hymne à l'Être Suprême* (1794) by François-Joseph Gossec. Beethoven was a great admirer of composers such as Cherubini, Grétry and Gossec, who were active during the revolution, and whose scores he would have seen in 1798 with the then French Ambassador in Vienna, Count Bernadotte. This Bernadotte would later become king of Sweden and Norway, and was one of the highly placed people who Beethoven approached in 1823 for support with the publication of the *Missa Solemnis*. In around 1800, Beethoven's enthusiasm for French revolutionary music began to bear its first fruits, for instance in the use of funeral marches (think of the slow movement of the *Sonata in C minor*, opus 13, *Pathétique*, or of the *Piano Sonata in A flat major*, opus 26), and a mixture of heroism and melancholy in some melodies (such as the Andante of the *Piano Sonata in D major*, opus 28). Apart from such obvious examples as the *Third Symphony* (*Eroica*) or the *Fifth Symphony*, the main theme of the *Violin Concerto* can also be seen as a result of this special relationship with French revolutionary music.

In addition to the myth of fate, there is evidently more to say about Beethoven's famous motif. This played an important role in an entirely different period of our culture, or should I say barbarity – namely, during the Second World War. Ta-ta-ta-daa, or short-short-short-long, is Morse code for the letter V for victory. In this way, Beethoven's symphony, already so rooted in revolution, was given an extra dimension as a symphony for freedom; as a symbol against the oppression of the Nazis. This shows once again how each product of the human brain that enters the public domain can become a plaything. Fortunately, this worked out well for the *Fifth*: as a revolutionary symphony for the freedom of us all. This fits it well.

It is worth noting, however, that the first performance of this symphony took place in entirely different circumstances. Napoleon created the Kingdom of Westphalia after the Treaty of Tilsit in 1807. His youngest brother, Jérôme Bonaparte, became king of the new dominion with a residence in Kassel. Jérôme was aware of his status as a foreigner, and made efforts to soften the negative mood by surrounding himself with a German court. For the post of *Kapellmeister* he invited Beethoven, a native Rheinlander. The conditions were extremely favourable for Beethoven, who was in constant financial need and had more enemies than friends in Vienna as a result of his blunt behaviour (partly the result of his increasing deafness, partly due to his indifference to any kind of etiquette).

That is why Beethoven accepted the offer without hesitation. He organised a farewell concert, which would take place on 22 December 1808 in the famous Theater an der Wien. Perhaps understandably, this concert turned out to be received in a less than welcome spirit by a large number of Beethoven's colleagues. Four years earlier he had dedicated his *Third Symphony* to Napoleon Bonaparte, but he subsequently removed the dedication when Napoleon had crowned himself Emperor and therefore undermined the most important ideals of the French Revolution: freedom, equality and brotherhood. Thus Beethoven was now colluding with the 'enemy'. How tense the situation became is revealed by the fact that the court *Kapellmeister* Salieri – the man who had set himself up as a fierce competitor of Mozart and later thwarted the ambitions of his pupil Franz Schubert – threatened to dismiss all of the musicians of the Imperial Court Orchestra who ventured to play for Beethoven's farewell concert, and this while Salieri had been giving lessons to Beethoven not long before, just after 1800.

That concert was a remarkable event in its own right. There were no fewer than six large works by Beethoven on the programme, enough for more than four hours of music, and that in December in an unheated hall. The audience was given successively the *Sixth Symphony* (*Pastorale*), the aria *Ah! perfido*, the Gloria from the *Mass in C*, the *Fourth Piano Concerto*, the *Fifth Symphony*, the Sanctus from the *Mass in C*, some improvisations given the title 'fantaisie' with the composer at the piano, and to finish, the *Fantasie* for piano, choir and orchestra. Beethoven's older colleague Johann Friedrich Reichardt later wrote that you can have too much of a good thing, especially if it is all loud. We can hardly imagine what that must have been like: an entire evening of music of which the ink was still wet, and finally that remarkable *Choral Fantasy* which Beethoven had composed at the last minute to be the brilliant finale to his farewell concert. According to the young composer Ignaz Moscheles, the piece was like a carriage riding down a hill at full speed. Something had to go wrong, and sure enough, the music derailed. The clarinets miscounted. Beethoven halted the performance and told the orchestra at which bar they should recommence, after which the music continued.

Thankfully, this engagement with Jérôme Bonaparte never went ahead. Even before Beethoven had packed his suitcases, indeed, even before the farewell concert had taken place, three wealthy and noble gentlemen – the princes Lobkowitz and Kinsky and Archduke Rudolph of Austria, the youngest brother of the Emperor – had offered him an annual stipend of four thousand florins in order to be able to work freely as a creative artist. The only condition set was that Beethoven had to remain in Vienna. Evidently, the 'farewell concert' went ahead, since a better opportunity for Beethoven to have his newest works heard wouldn't come around again soon, even without reviews. In addition, he didn't have to move house. The contract was signed on 1st March 1809, even though Beethoven actually considered the amount rather on the low side. But many Viennese families had to live on less.

The amount of four thousand florins was fixed at the value of banknotes that had a fluctuating rate against the then Austrian guilder. Within a year the rate had dropped by half, and in 1811 there was only twenty per cent left. Austria was on the brink of bankruptcy. In the meantime, Vienna had been occupied by Napoleon's troops, as a result of which Beethoven had annotated the sketches of his *Fifth Piano Concerto* with cries of 'Auf der Schlacht. Jubelgesang!', 'Angriff' en 'Sieg!' During the siege of the city he entrenched himself in the cellar with his brother Carl, with his head under thick cushions. The *Seventh Symphony* was given its first performance on 8th December 1813, during a special benefit concert for Austrian and Bavarian soldiers wounded at Hanau in the battle against the Napoleonic troops, who were retreating from Russia.

This concert also saw the launch of Beethoven's most remarkable orchestral work, namely *Wellingtons Sieg, oder die Schlacht bei Vittoria*. In this piece the French and English armies battle each other near this small northern Spanish town. From one side come the troops of the Duke of Wellington, accompanied by the martial song *Rule Britannia*, and on the other side those of Joseph Bonaparte, the then King of Spain, introduced by the popular French song *Malborough s'en va-t-en guerre*. Moreover, Beethoven has both armies enter the stage represented by a battalion of drummers and trumpeters who challenge each other with the usual signals. Then the battle commences: the entire engagement including attack marches, the defeat of the French and final victory. Beethoven himself saw this work as an occasional piece without further merit, but the audience loved it just as much as they had the *Seventh Symphony*.

Both works were repeated successfully within a few months. This gave the directors of the imperial opera the idea to revive the not very successful opera *Leonore*, but Beethoven decided to revise this into *Fidelio*. *Leonore,* alias *Fidelio,* is about oppression and freedom. Florestan is a nobleman who has been imprisoned and is being starved in the dungeons of his rival, the tyrannical Pizarro. Florestan's wife Leonore has disguised herself as a man, Fidelio (the faithful), and has managed to enter the service of the prison guard Rocco in order to reach Florestan. At the end of the opera, the soldiers of the minister, Don Fernando, arrive just in time, and Florestan is freed from the hands of Pizarro. Tyranny is driven out, just as Napoleon had also been defeated (although the Battle of Waterloo was still needed for a definitive conclusion). Beethoven's theme was therefore directly linked to the general mood at the time, as was also true of his great symphonies, and in particular the uneven-numbered ones, starting with the *Eroica*.

Let's return to the *Fifth Symphony*. The most important movement of this symphony is not in fact the first, and this score is also about much more than that signal: the four notes of the opening. The signal works as an impulse, a source of energy, for everything that follows. In physics this would be called an 'induction', and with it Beethoven empowers the entire composition. The main theme of the first movement grows directly from it, and it is the basis from which the whole symphony is subsequently forged. Never before had Beethoven worked so economically in a composition. The ta-ta-ta-daa (see fig. 12a) returns as a rhythm in the second movement, the Andante con moto, as a starting point of the musical sentence (see fig. 12b), and also further on as an accompanying figure with descending notes, subtly hidden so that it doesn't stand out, but is something that you feel (see fig. 12c). A variant can be found in the Scherzo in the horns: this time not with three light accents as a preliminary to the heavy 'daa', but with an accent on the first short 'ta', making it into a sort of miniature waltz, Tá-ta-ta-Daa, with the Daa equal in length to the three short 'tas' put together (see fig. 12d).

The most surprising of Beethoven's inventions is also to be found in this Scherzo. After a somewhat rugged trio, the music from the beginning of this movement returns extremely softly, even at one point played pizzicato (plucked) by the strings. The effect of this is that you are left wondering where it is going, what is going to happen. The music becomes completely calm, and then, from that calm and as if you had landed in the eye of a storm, Beethoven balls so much energy together that the triumphal finale seems to emerge from it as if inevitably. Only then are the piccolo, the double bassoon and the three trombones brought into action: radiant and festive. It now turns out that everything we have heard until this moment, even the ta-ta-ta-daa, has been no more than a prelude to this grand finale; since here, too, we also hear a variant of that famous little motif (see fig. 12e). This finale is the ultimate aim of the symphony. This is the centre of gravity. Therefore we sometimes refer to the *Fifth* as a 'finale symphony', of which it has been a model for almost all of the great symphonies of the 19th century.

Apparently Beethoven was very pleased with this transition from the Scherzo to the finale; since, in the middle of this finale he momentarily repeats the effect and does something extremely unusual: he brings back the Scherzo in the middle of the last movement of the symphony. And, if that were not enough, he has another exciting surprise in store just before the finish, in the coda, the final 'tail' of this movement and therefore of the entire symphony. Suddenly the music moves into high gear and the attack is set in motion. Accompanied by two basic elements, a kind of army drum rhythm (daa-ta-da-ta-ta-ta) and the ta-ta-ta-daa

12. Ludwig van Beethoven, *Fifth Symphony*.

from the first movement, the music sweeps towards the end. Indeed, it has all the appearance of a military *blitzkrieg*, and Beethoven seems not to know where to stop. The final chord, in a radiant C major as a victory over the more dramatic C minor, is really hammered home.

However, perhaps Beethoven was less original than we would like to see him. This entire coda can be found as an idea, with the same speeding up, in the overture to Cherubini's opera *Eliza* (1794), performed in Vienna in 1803. In Cherubini's hands it sounds nice, but with Beethoven it becomes exceptionally driven and thrilling. The compact forms and sophisticated structures are matched by exciting motivic developments, harmonies and rhythms. Beethoven's music never slackens, keeping the listener constantly on the edge of their seat and thrusting them into its adventure. Apollonian and Dionysian go hand in hand and ensure that here, as in so many of Beethoven's other works, the true nature of the tragedy in this symphony is revealed.

Nonetheless, Beethoven's *Fifth Symphony* was not an immediate success at its first performance on 22 December 1808. People didn't really know what to do with it, and it would actually take a long time before the work could really be appreciated. At the beginning, the *Fifth* never enjoyed the swift and continued success of the *Seventh*. Even in 1828, when it was performed for the first time in Paris, many were shocked by the intensity of this music. The young Hector Berlioz wrote about it in his memoires. After a first performance on 13 April 1828 by the orchestra of the Société des Concerts du Conservatoire, he persuaded his teacher Jean-François Lesueur to go with him to the next performance a few weeks later. Berlioz met him afterwards in the corridor.

> He was red as a beetroot and walking with big strides. 'And, dear master?' I asked him. – 'Ouf! I'm going outside; I need some fresh air. It is inconceivable, amazing! It's turned me upside down and so confused me that when I left my seat and went to put on my hat I thought I wouldn't be able to find my

head! Leave me alone. Until tomorrow...' I triumphed. The next day I hurried to find him. Straight away the discussion was about the masterpiece that had so excited us. Lesueur let me talk for a time, while he calmly acknowledged my adoring exclamations. You could easily see that I no longer had the same man in front of me for whom on the previous evening this subject had been too painful. I carried on however, until Lesueur, from whom I had managed to coax a glimpse of the great emotions he had shown when hearing Beethoven's symphony, said to me while shaking his head and giving a strange smile: 'Whatever is the case, people shouldn't make that sort of music.' To which I replied, 'Rest assured, dear master, that will not happen often.'

Within a generation, Beethoven's *Fifth* was widely acknowledged as a masterpiece. For almost the entire duration of the 19th century, composers felt the hot breath of Beethoven's genius on their necks when staring at their blank manuscript paper and awaiting inspiration. Schumann and Brahms recognised Beethoven as a progenitor of their music, with Bach as its primal father. Soon after Beethoven's death the *Fifth* became mythologised and the signal motif transformed into the symbol of fate knocking on the door. This image suited that of Beethoven's suffering, on which his followers laid so much emphasis. In addition to this, pathetic composers are harmless. 'It is only Beethoven, that deaf man. That's why he speaks much too loudly.' Such remarks can be found in the reports of the Viennese secret police, who regarded him as a clown rather than a politically dangerous individual. His *Fifth Symphony*, however, is indeed the work of a revolutionary spirit, at least if we seek to hear the context that contributed to the basis of Beethoven's inspiration.

And those four opening notes? We can only be amazed at how a composer could create such a majestic work with something so trivial as those four notes and that single rhythm, which had been tried by so many before. This requires not so much courage, not expressly a revolutionary temperament, but above all an incredible power of spirit, a great deal of self-confidence and a willingness for the fight. With Prometheus as his fiery trademark, Beethoven knew that man would have remained a cave dweller without that spiritual fire of intelligence. With the *Fifth* as *pars pro toto* for his entire oeuvre, he demonstrated what the human brain is able to achieve.

14. Classical music

In the world of music we invariably talk about 'classical music', by which we mean something other than pop, commercial or folk music. The term classical music is somewhat confusing, however; after all, what do we mean by classical, and in our case classical music? 'Classical,' as defined by most dictionaries, such as the most recent Merriam-Webster, is among other definitions: 1. relating to Greek or Roman antiquity; 2. exemplary of its kind, serving as a model to which permanent authority can be ascribed. Sometimes the following definition is added: 'stemming from earlier times and yet not outdated: *classical music*.' And 'classical music' leads to a separate indication: 'that of the great composers of the 17th, 18th and 19th centuries' or 'relating to, or being music in the educated European tradition that includes such forms as art song, chamber music, opera, and symphony as distinguished from folk or popular music or jazz.'

The first definition of 'classical' is not much use to us. There is of course a certain amount of knowledge about the music of the ancient Greeks and Romans, but this plays virtually no role in our times, not in terms of sound and even less as a point of reference. This has no relevance to the term 'classical music' as used by us on a daily basis. We therefore have to try the second definition: exemplary of its kind. But who decides this? For example, which music is exemplary? Which composers are to be included? Generally we think of Mozart or Beethoven as exemplary composers of classical music. Schoenberg and Stravinsky, on the other hand, count as representatives of modern music, and Pierre Boulez and Louis Andriessen of contemporary music. But do they not write 'classical' music, too?

It becomes even more confusing when we distinguish a 'Classical period', namely that of the Viennese classical composers: Haydn, Mozart and Beethoven. And even more so when in art history the first sixty years of the so-called Classical period, which is roughly situated between 1740 and 1820, is regarded as 'Classicism', with the term meaning 'following the classics', and the subsequent period (from about 1815) as 'Romantic'. In architecture, on the other hand, it is acknowledged that there was already a strong leaning towards the use of examples from Classical Antiquity from the late 15th century. Why shouldn't this trend be equally traceable with composers of the time? But we have to bear in mind that this terminology, as much in the visual arts as in literature and music, was established only in the 19th century and has remained unchanged ever since, often against our better judgement.

We use the same terms next to each other in a cultural historical sense as well as in determining standard norms. On the one hand, we consider Mozart to be a composer from the Classical period, and on the other, his music is invoked as a classic example of Western art music. The latter is to a certain extent justified, as most scientists and even more music lovers agree that it would hardly be possible to find better music. In this sense, however, we can also place numerous great masters from the past and present under the term 'classic', including names such as Josquin des Prez, Palestrina, Monteverdi, Purcell, Bach, Beethoven, Brahms, Debussy, Bartók, and even Webern, Boulez and others. Or is that not the case? For many, their music is equally exemplary. However, the term classic is also quite uninformative, as in 'classic' wallpaper, 'classic' cars and a 'classic' bicycle race: classic in the sense of being widely recognised. For that matter, are the songs of The Beatles, Barbra Streisand, David Bowie or Nina Hagen also not classic?

This confusion is even doubled when it comes to Haydn and Mozart. Are they Classical composers or classicist? They are classic in the sense that their music is counted as part of the Classical period, and they are classicist because their music shows, as one often reads, 'flawlessness of form and the search for harmonic proportions which remind us of the attitudes of the classical ancients.' A frequent addendum to this is that a classicist repertoire of forms is applied in the works of Haydn and Mozart, but what is this repertoire? Are these forms based

13. Victor Tilgner, *Mozart-Denkmal* (1896), Vienna (in its original location: Albertinaplatz, photo ca 1900).

on those of architecture? No, this is emphatically not the case. The music of the late 18th century is above all concerned with sonata, binary and ternary forms which, it has to be said, are mostly quite balanced in structure. This, however, is where any comparison with classical architecture ends. In the works of Haydn and Mozart, form and content do not have the same aim or effect. The form has to do with the placement of the material in time and structure, the content is largely determined by the nature of the material. Violently dissonant harmonies, propulsive melodies and dynamic contrasts are sooner romantic than classicistic, even when these are brought together in a balanced form.

It is no less confusing that classicism in French culture is situated around 1700 and not in Haydn's and Mozart's time, while in architecture classical forms were already being employed in the 16th century. Still following? No one can, in fact, though attempts have been made. With regard to music, Charles Rosen wrote a fine book on the subject, *The Classical Style* (1972), though Mozart would probably have laughed heartily at its arguments. Mozart had nothing to do with nor was he interested in the antique world, except perhaps when there were useful stories to be found for his operas, full of heroes and demigods. The term 'classicism' didn't even exist in his time. 'Being Classical' was certainly not his goal as a composer.

In 1810 the German author and composer E.T.A. Hoffmann wrote in a review of Beethoven's *Fifth Symphony* that Haydn, Mozart and Beethoven 'breathed the same romantic spirit' with their instrumental works, in the sense that they understood the essence of art in the same way. 'Mozart takes us into the depths of the spirit. Fear envelops us.' A few years later in 1813, in *Der Dichter und der Komponist*, he did talk about Mozart's 'classical' operas, but strictly in a normative sense. Indeed, Mozart's music had already been held up as a norm, as had that of Haydn, though to a lesser degree. This was mainly due to the fact that in Haydn's music, Hoffmann and many of his contemporaries heard the good cheer and playfulness of happy people, while in his opinion Mozart and Beethoven explored the dark side of the human spirit. Even during his lifetime, Mozart's music was regarded as remarkably expressive and also confusing.

The transformation of Mozart from a romantic spirit into a white angel during the 19th century is another story. It is clear, however, that in the 21st century we are stuck with a barely adequate and largely 19th-century terminology. In addition, could we actually say that the compositions of Schubert, Chopin, Ravel, Bartók or Boulez are not 'flawless of form', or not constructed according to 'harmonic proportions' in ways that would make us think about visions of Classical Antiquity? And isn't the music of Josquin des Prez and Palestrina at least as classical as that of Mozart? Apparently not, since in many reference books the term 'classical music' is limited to the 17th, 18th, and 19th centuries. In recent editions this time limit has often been removed, but as a result the term 'classical music' means even less: 'stemming from earlier times and yet not outdated.'

Everyday usage seems to indicate that anything which is not pop or folk music, and that cannot be put in the category of music for entertainment or advertising, is quickly categorised as 'classical music': what in German studies is so concisely termed 'serious music' (*Ernste Musik*). This provides us with another problem. A great deal is lumped together under the heading 'classical music' which is neither exemplary nor reckoned as part of the supposed Classical period, but at the very most as Western art music, in other words, notated music which is intended for performance in one way or another. The term 'classical music' is thus a true repository of styles, techniques and qualities. In fact, this is everything which sounds more or less familiar to us, which has the appearance of everything we have already canonised: which sounds like Bach, Mozart or Beethoven, like Brahms or Mahler. Comparatively, Franz Berwald belongs as equally to classical music as Jean Richafort or Wilhelm Stenhammar, and as much as Guillaume de Machaut or Johannes Ciconia. We are, slowly but surely, also increasingly tempted to count The Beatles as part of the classical music realm.

We cannot operate easily with the term 'classical music'. So what then should we use? Art music, as opposed to folk music, for instance? Or music art – as opposed to the arts of painting or poetry? The former is rather snobbish, and the latter sounds awkward. These things are a question of becoming acclimatised, but the problem remains. In short, we will keep classical music for the time being, while knowing how relative, levelling and often meaningless this term is. This is fortunately in contradiction to the many remarkable compositions which are served up to us as classical music on a daily basis, and at least as many which are not included, but which in fact are no less classical.

15. Hearing, listening and remembering

In order to experience music we have to be able to hear it, since without this it does not exist as an acoustic phenomenon. Music first has to sound in order to be heard, but even then, that 'being heard' is only half the battle. We also have to listen actively; yes, even listen closely. In *Toscanini and Debussy, the magic of reality* (*Toscanini en Debussy, magie der werkelijkheid*), the Dutch composer Rudolf Escher stressed the need for careful listening: 'The "wonders" of any music will never be "revealed" if this doesn't happen in a natural way: sounding and listening. *Good* sounding and *good* listening. The second is instantly impossible when the first is not fulfilled.' While good listening is a task for the audience, sounding good is in the first instance the responsibility of the composer, subsequently that of the performing musician, and finally that of various environmental factors.

That which the composer invents must be able to sound in order to be audible to the listener in a pure physical sense, otherwise communication of any kind is impossible. For example, a softly played piccolo amidst a couple of loud trumpets and trombones results in the piccolo not being heard. The experience of seeing a musician playing in an orchestra but not being able to hear the sound of their instrument is not uncommon. Is this the fault of the composer who has orchestrated his piece badly, that of the musicians themselves, or the conductor who hasn't managed to find the correct balance, the acoustics of the hall, or the listener who might be mildly deaf to higher frequencies, or is it a combination of these different factors? As long as the composer understands his trade then the most important condition is met, and under the right conditions the music can sound good.

With the composing and performance of music and the subsequent listening experience, the transmitter and receiver of music have to be coordinated optimally. No less important are the acoustics of the space, the quality of the instruments being played, any number of possible ambient sounds and even the temperature or humidity in a room, which has its effect on the sound of the instruments and the acoustics, and – when required – the nature of the amplification. If environmental factors hamper listening or pollute the sound, the result can be compared with looking at a painting by Van Gogh in a badly-lit room, through smoke-filled air or through spectacles with green or red lenses. The intentions of the painter can never come across correctly under these circumstances. Even if we look carefully, we still won't be able to see the work properly.

Imagine a small string ensemble accompanied by a harpsichord playing in the corner of a beautiful salon. If in the same room there is a crowd of people having a drink and an animated conversation, then only those standing in the immediate vicinity of the ensemble will be able to experience more of the music than just a few loose fragments. Haydn or Mozart would have encountered this on numerous occasions. In a museum, you can move around someone who is standing between you and a work of art and barring your line of sight. From your new position you can once again try and see the painting in its entirety. By contrast, an acoustic disturbance in the concert hall can only be erased by listening to the entire piece anew from the first bar. 'Hey, can you play that movement again? Someone sneezed/coughed/was talking next to me and I missed a couple of bars...'; as if a piece had been cut out of the painting.

At this point, I want to return to the quote by Rudolf Escher, but now with its continuation. This provides an important insight into music as a temporal art.

> On music rests the doom of transience. While sounding it goes by and is *over*. For a limited time our memory is capable of relating a past sound to a present sound, but with the onset of silence (and *what* a silence, often what a transformed silence!), there is nothing left of that intangible 'construction.' Neither

the ability to remember melodies, fragments, even the entire work (it is after all possible to retain this perfectly in one's head), nor the ability to talk about the work, or to read it by using the score, can remedy that lack of reality.

As Escher points out, a musical experience cannot be had without memory. We have to be able to remember what we have just heard, but in the moment that a sound enters our consciousness and that we perceive what we have heard, that same sound that we have just heard is already gone. Without memory we are not capable of bringing what we have heard into relation with what we are hearing. This of course applies to all art forms which elapse over time, such as film, theatre or dance, but it is good to bear this in mind, since it has consequences for all participants: for composers, performing musicians and listeners.

Why is there so much repetition in so much music? This is not necessarily a stylistic phenomenon, such as in repetitive or *minimal* music. The greater aim is that at least we remember what we have heard. Even with a good memory, this is not always simple. Why, then, must performing musicians give a useful meaning to all these repetitions? Mainly to avoid the feeling that we are hearing the same thing again after two repeats; after all, what has sounded previously is given a different meaning because of the modified context created by new material. Since each repetition is furthermore connected with the previous one, it is therefore coloured by it. The composer and performing musician must make this extra clear to us. This is comparable with repetitions in nature which seem the same, but which in reality are often just a little different. Despite these natural variations, we can form a consistent image of the world around us. In music, too, our memory must be fed by repetitions in order to be able to follow it and experience it as a unified whole.

Moreover, Escher points out that even when our memory is perfectly fine, remembering music has no effect on the reality or the physical experience of music, which is eternally absent when it no longer sounds. What we all too frequently recall is not the music itself in all its details, but the experience we had at the moment of listening, the feelings we underwent, the emotions and a multitude of environmental factors (who you were sitting next to, what your associations were when listening, which scents you smelt and so on), and of course parts of the music itself, once we have come to know it better; as sounding memory or remembered sound. This only comes with careful listening, however, and that is our primary task as music lovers.

16. On composing

When we think of music composition as the invention of music in general then the term covers everything, including music that has been handed down through centuries-old oral traditions. Everything which emerges from the human brain is in a certain sense 'invented' and 'made up', and thus composed, even if it is not always written down. At the same time, this also encapsulates the riddle of composing. How is such an abstract expression as music thought up? Where do the sounds that a composer invents come from? Is it merely inspiration? Or is there more to the process of composition?

The mysteries of inspiration have been discussed previously. Nevertheless, I would like to approach the subject of composing here, even though it is mainly a personal vision. This cannot be otherwise. Numerous composers have tried to explain or put into words their way of working, but the moments at which the best and most beautiful musical thoughts emerge from their pen or computer remain an enigma. Were they inspired or did they inspire themselves? Did the Holy Spirit descend upon them: *Veni creator spiritus*...? Or did they evoke numerous thoughts and ideas in themselves, which eventually led to a composition created through skill and hard work? Is inspiration really that important for a successful creation? Should one wait for it, or does it have to be enforced? If the former is represented by a dove, as the symbol of the Holy Spirit, then in the latter we can imagine Moses, who beat a rock with a stick until water began to flow.

In an earlier chapter I referred to the symbol of the dove on the shoulder of Pope Gregory: the Holy Spirit helping the Church Father while creating the liturgical melodies which were given his name, Gregorian chant or plainchant. Fiction or reality, very few artists have been able to put the miracle of creative revelation into words. Paul Hindemith wrote the following about this in 1952, in *A Composer's World. Horizons and Limitations*:

> We all know the impression of a very heavy flash of lightning in the night. Within a second's time we see a broad landscape, not only in its general outlines but with every detail. Although we could never describe each single component of the picture, we feel that not even the smallest leaf of grass escapes our attention.
>
> We experience a view, immensely comprehensive and at the same time immensely detailed, that we never could have under normal daylight conditions, and perhaps not during the night either, if our senses and nerves were not strained by the extraordinary suddenness of the event. Compositions must be conceived the same way. [...] It is obvious that a composer, during the long period the notation of his work requires, is always in danger of losing the original vision of it.

Hindemith makes a distinction here between the creative spark and the actual craft that follows, between inspiration and transpiration, between idea and form. He also makes clear that this inspiration has to have great strength in order to be sustained during the sometimes long process of working out, fixing and giving shape to a work. This hard work is of course easier for one composer than for another. One does almost everything in his head and copies his composition directly onto manuscript or digital paper. The other sketches and rejects with a vengeance, thereby providing us with a glimpse behind the scenes as to how the music is made. Some composers simply have a better memory than others. Some composers feel more at ease with a piano or a sheet of paper within reach, others do not.

At the peak of our Western musical culture, we can find composers on the one hand who endlessly sketched in booklets and on large sheets of manuscript paper (thinking of Beethoven or Mahler), and on the other hand, composers from whom we have much less written evidence, who probably prepared a great deal of their work in advance in their heads before putting pen to paper (Bach, Mozart and Schubert). This latter group give the impression that they were able to write their music directly into neat copy as if out of nowhere, but this is an illusion. Many a composer discarded his sketches on completion of the work, or this may have been done by his descendants after his death. When composers such as Bach, Mozart and Schubert left sketches – and by this I mean extensive sketches, with every phase of an idea, all possible options and much crossing out – then there was apparently something special going on. These were struggles with form or with themes, with a remarkable combination of instruments or the search for something of which they themselves had only a vague idea, something which slumbered somewhere in the subconscious and needed to be teased out through hard work.

A good memory can certainly facilitate the gift of composing, precisely because music is a temporal art and the composer has to know exactly where he is in the process of writing at every moment in his work. Even notorious sketchers such as Beethoven had an above-average memory. One example of an exceptional

14. Wolfgang Amadeus Mozart, page from the *Overture* to *Don Giovanni*, autograph, in the Bibliothèque nationale de France in Paris.

achievement in this area is given by Mozart who, as he once wrote to his sister Nannerl, copied a movement from a work from memory while at the same time composing another movement. Mozart also had fairy tales read to him for an entire night (on the eve of the première of *Don Giovanni* in Prague) in order not to fall asleep while writing out the overture of the opera from memory.

Sometimes a composer has to hold onto musical ideas for months or even years, and be able to oversee the numerous variants of these ideas next to each other in order to steer the step-by-step development of the material – and then not only with a single line or melody, but across multiple simultaneously-sounding layers. The desired result in performance is to give the impression that the music created itself, that it was effortlessly entrusted to paper and appeared as if by magic. The composer has to have one foot hard on the accelerator, driven forward by the power of his ideas and constantly refreshed inspiration, and with his other foot equally hard on the brake in order to be able to capture everything, down to the smallest details, over longer periods of time.

Let's return to that moment of the flash of lightning, a fascinating moment in the creative process. So much energy, willpower and imagination has to spring from it in order for everything else to become possible. The flywheel of inspiration has to be set in motion and needs to keep running. The eternal question which composers ask themselves is how to call on this inspiration, that bolt of lightning, that single spark, that one idea which sets everything in motion. Wouldn't we love to be able to summon inspiration at will? Yet it seems that for most of the time inspiration overcomes us, that – to use that image once again – the Holy Spirit gives us a helping hand at unexpected moments. Are appearances deceptive? Is that one inspired brainwave really so essential for the success of a composition?

Some years ago, Matthew Guerrieri wrote a fascinating and comprehensive study dedicated exclusively to the first four notes of the first movement of Beethoven's *Fifth Symphony*: those four remarkably unremarkable notes about which I already wrote in a previous chapter. What Beethoven did with these four notes borders on the incredible. However, those first four notes are, as can be seen in the sketchbooks, anything but the result of a single moment of sublime inspiration. Only after a number of fruitless attempts and failed beginnings did that little motif appear in its final form. Beethoven wrought, compelled and forged it step by step. He had to work hard for it.

Was this what Hindemith meant to say? Or is it not about that flash of lightning, but rather about the landscape that has been illuminated by it for a millisecond? The sudden awareness of overseeing an entire work? Translated to the craft of composing, the foremost essence is in the reconstruction of that briefly visible landscape. What material is needed for this? Which choices have to be made? The achievement is not made with inspiration alone, any more than it is with talent alone. The composer literally has to do what is in his title: composing, compiling, editing, which implies manipulating time and travelling through an as yet non-existent composition. He must organise his material in order ultimately to be able to play with the mood of his listeners, to demand attention and to communicate, and that with the most abstract means there are: sounds structured in time; notes on paper.

Once he has made a start, what is the composer to rely on? Which means, which techniques can he use? How did Josquin des Prez, Monteverdi, Bach, Mozart, Beethoven, Wagner or Debussy, Hindemith or Pierre Boulez go from A to B, from the first to the last bar in a composition? How did they arrive at a rounded musical product from that very first idea? Many scholarly studies have been written on this, in which academics diligently elaborate on their suspicions about the creative processes of numerous composers. Even when composers have opened the book on their own way of working, the core aspects remain shrouded in mystery: for us, and not infrequently for the composers themselves.

In 1951 Arthur Honegger wrote candidly on this in *Je suis compositeur*, comparing his work with the creation of a ladder, without being able to support it against a wall or even some scaffolding.

> The building under construction remains in balance only through the miracle of some kind of internal logic, from an inner sense of proportion. I am simultaneously the architect and observer of my work: I work and watch. If I encounter an unexpected obstacle I leave my work desk, sit in the chair of the listener and ask myself, 'What, after having heard that which went previously, would I now like to hear: what would give me, if not the shudder of creation, at least the impression of success? What would logically have to follow to satisfy me?' So I try to find that follow-up, not with a banal formula which can be seen by everyone, but using a new element which stimulates interest. Following this method, my score grows bit by bit.

For many a composer these flashes of inspiration seem to appear suddenly, falling unsolicited into their lap or coming to them almost imperceptibly. Doubts about the correct way to arrive at a musical work of art have only increased, despite attempts in the past century to engage human intelligence more consciously with the creative process, or even to involve computers. There are now so many possibilities, so many techniques and musical languages from which to choose.

Until well into the 19th century musical material and musical language were unambiguous. There was debate about style, about the content and nature of the musical narrative, or about the function of a piece of music, but hardly any debate about the material itself. Music theory changed only incrementally. As long as the principles of a piece of music are clear to everyone and subject to very little change, then there is still plenty of room for a personal touch or vision within the existing frameworks, for an artistic signature which is immediately recognisable. 'Dialects' in music were therefore able to arise from the earliest times: local content given to a basic principle. This, for instance, is an explanation as to why the same liturgical chant, spread from Rome, had so many variants in the many monasteries across Europe.

The personal touch for which the composer strove after the 15th century was determined by individual colouration over an otherwise consistent basis. Through these colourations we can recognise Josquin des Prez, Monteverdi, Purcell, Bach, Haydn, Mozart, Beethoven, Verdi, Wagner, Stravinsky, Alban Berg and many others. Piece by piece, they uttered their musical thoughts from within a remarkably universal language. Individualism became an increasingly important objective within Western European culture after the Renaissance. This is still the case, although after the Second World War many authors opposed this concept and considered the dream of the Enlightenment to be a dead end.

From the point of view of the composer, we can agree that for a long time a recognisable, universal musical language existed with a fixed set of rules which were only adjusted or changed on a few points over the course of many centuries. This allowed a composer to be entirely himself in his creative work. If he had personality, was capable of delivering a recognisable narrative, and of course if he had mastered the technical aspects of composing to the last details, then all he had to do was make sure that what he had invented was written down on paper. Everything that had not previously been thought or said, everything that had not previously sounded as such, was received by the public directly as something new. For as composer, stretching proven techniques is a great deal simpler than inventing new ones.

Even then, it was sometimes difficult for even the best composers to penetrate into the core of their being. Fortunately, they could concentrate entirely on that inner quest by relying fully on their technical abilities. Consciously or unconsciously, in doing so they were able to act as custodians of the difference between their inner thoughts and those ideas which made their way from the outside world. Ultimately, you do not want to be influenced too much by others, but it is almost impossible to isolate yourself entirely from what is around you. What the composer hears inwardly, he can only realise beyond his consciousness by playing it himself, provided he is able to do so, or by writing it down via a compromise, namely in a notation based on symbols. When he subsequently re-absorbs the music (by reading the symbols, playing the music or listening to it in performed sound), he renders a different content of consciousness to what is heard, which often merges imperceptibly with his original content of consciousness. Thus there is always an interaction between the inner and outer world.

The extent to which a composer could rely on his technical mastery of the trade can be seen in a letter which Mozart wrote in September 1790 from Frankfurt to his wife Constanze: 'If people were able to see into my heart then I would almost be ashamed, – everything inside is cold, ice cold.' Mozart is talking about a fascinating phenomenon. He could compose anything which was asked of him or that entered his mind, but he was not always enthusiastic in equal measure, and it did not always give him much pleasure. At such times his mind went on composing independently, with all of the required technical demands in place, but his heart wasn't in it. In a similar way, Richard Strauss once let slip that he kept his writing hand in good condition by just writing notes on a daily basis. In all of this it is striking that a mastery of craftsmanship and the uniformity of the basic language have helped to ensure that composers could – to use a neologism – sometimes almost work on autopilot. They relied entirely on their technique.

The downside of such an approach is that the personality of the artist, the individual touch and power of the discourse can be relegated to the background. This argument, however, only applies in times that individual personality is seen as an essential criterion for the quality of art. For composers who are entirely focused on the technical craftsmanship in their work, and for whom personal artistic expression is not an end in itself, as was the case for almost every composer before 1600, individuality is no more than a pleasant but dispensable side-effect. In fact it is precisely the particular way in which each of them deals with the general technical rules which distinguishes them from others. In addition, personality is not something you can learn, whereas the vocational skills of a craft can be acquired. You have personality or you don't. I can therefore also state, as did Mahler: you can compose, or you can't.

Let's return to the handwork of the composer. 'Where to begin?' is the question many composers ask themselves when they are sitting in front of a blank sheet of paper. Does one start with a melody, a motif or some harmonies, or indeed with a set system, a structure? Everything depends on the nature of the initial idea. No idea, no thought is identical to another. Essentially it is a question of whether you start with the form or the content, with technique or the 'soft landing' of an inspired idea. Whether you first create a system and then start working with that, or the system is distilled from the ideas. Some composers need a structure or system before they can commence work; others seek one or more musical ideas that will eventually determine the most appropriate form or structure.

The one lets himself be led by the music and runs after it with his musical divining rod, the other forms and shapes and builds his work of art stone by stone. There are composers who begin neatly with the first bars of a new opus and steadily work towards the end. Often though, what originally looked like the first bars of a piece in reality appear at its the end or somewhere in the middle. Many first ideas turn out, after much work, to lead to nothing other than different new ideas, which in their turn lead to still more ideas. And then suddenly there is an arrival – eureka! – and the flywheel of creativity starts spinning like mad.

With all of this there are a few things that have proven their worth over the centuries, especially now we are capable of looking from one musical mountain peak to the other, with a view on a large number of successes from the past. It is not that one idea, that theme, motif or series of particular harmonies that make a composition unique, but what a composer has done with these. For this one needs formative insight, narrative skill and above all fantasy in order to avoid falling into repetition within a longer time span. The continuous varying of material is a true art. All of the great masters since the 14th century, from Guillaume de Machaut, via Guillaume Dufay and Josquin des Prez, Claudio Monteverdi, Heinrich Schütz, Henry Purcell, Johann Sebastian Bach, Wolfgang Amadeus Mozart, Franz Schubert, Johannes Brahms, Claude Debussy and Igor Stravinsky, to Benjamin Britten, Pierre Boulez and Tristan Keuris, Steve Reich, Arvo Pärt and Simeon ten Holt, understood the art of variation and transformation.

Formative insight is of importance because composing is not a 'filling-in' exercise but a 'filling-out' one, or in other words, the chosen material and its possibilities ultimately determine which form suits it the best, and which emerges from the material in the most logical way. However, should you still want to work with a previously established form, this will also have direct consequences for your choice of the material which eventually will have to find a place in that particular form. You cannot build a house from eggshells, nor can you make a necklace from bricks. Schubert's seemingly endless melodies in his great *Symphony in C major* and those by Bruckner in his *Seventh Symphony* had consequences for the size of these orchestral works, and the concise possibilities of the twelve-tone series chosen by Anton Webern in his *Symphony* ultimately determined the barely nine-and-a-half-minute duration of the entire work.

The art of narration is of course particularly connected with the transmission of music, with its communication to the listener. This is not to say that music always has to tell a 'story'. Technique by itself can be sufficient as a narrative, too. After all, the way in which melodies, harmonies, rhythms and everything else which determines the sound of music are strung together, combined and led through time, is no less a story than 'once upon a time' or

'Ave Maria'. This is in fact all about the many manifestations of musical rhetoric. For example, one of the most successful musical structures is sonata form, which took flight from the middle of the 18th century and can be found in innumerable sonatas, quartets, symphonies and concertos. Sonata form is frequently connected to musical classicism, but in reality the principle of musical dialectic (with two contrasting themes and with many harmonic modulations in the heart of these compositions) is unquestionably the result of a desire to write stimulating, narrative music which can also be enjoyed by the man in the street ('without their understanding how', to paraphrase the words of Leopold Mozart to his son). Its Apollonian form therefore houses Dionysian content.

The aforementioned notions and techniques have been decisive for a large part of composition in Western culture up to the middle of the last century. There are of course many more things that a composer has to know and be capable of in order to realise his dreams, to be able to draw his listeners along or hold up a mirror to them. Nowadays, the possibilities are endless. Nevertheless, the number of composers who have these abilities remains limited.

Part D

17. Dvořák and the Bohemian overcoat

'We have here in America been offered a pattern for an "American" national musical costume by the Bohemian Dvořák – though what Negro melodies have to do with Americanism in

15. Antonin Dvořák

art still remains a mystery.' That was telling him: a Bohemian costume for Americans indeed! This statement comes from the American composer Edward MacDowell, whose two piano concertos incidentally sound very much like those of the Norwegian Edvard Grieg. Never mind, you don't always have to be capable of practising what you preach. From 1896 MacDowell was the first professor at the faculty of music at Columbia University. He had studied in Europe, in Paris and Frankfurt. Alternatives were yet to be established in the United States. Nationalism had little to do with folk music for MacDowell. However, by contrast, Antonín Dvořák had propagated the use of melodies of Native Americans and African Americans some years before as a way of achieving a national American music.

Dvořák arrived in the United States at the end of September 1892 on a steamer from Bremen, accompanied by his wife and two of his six children. The purpose of his trip was two-fold. He had a desire to study American music, but he had also been invited by the wealthy Mrs Jeanette Thurber to take up the post as director of the new National Conservatory of Music of America in New York, which she was financing. Dvořák described his duties in a letter to a friend: 'The directorship of the Conservatoire and to conduct 10 concerts (with my own compositions) for 8 months and 4 months vacation, for a salary of 15,000 dollars or over 30,000 gold francs. Should I take it? Or should I not?' Of course, he didn't refuse. He would never have been able to earn that much money in Prague, and in addition Mrs Thurber had arranged everything so that he could continue composing. The new post represented both his reward and recognition.

Dvořák wrote several famous works in America, including the *String Quartet in F major*, also known as the 'American' and previously even the 'Negro' quartet, and the *Symphony in E minor*, with the title *From the New World*. The most fascinating part of Dvořák's journey, however, is his study of American music. Was that pure curiosity or a clever move to make his position more acceptable to the Americans? What would Dvořák have considered to be American music? If we are to rely on the evidence of the new symphony, which he had largely completed within six months of his arrival in New York, Dvořák was inspired above all by the romantic-epic poem by Longfellow about the fictional hero Hiawatha, by his contacts with some musicians from the black community in New York who taught him several spirituals, and by the 'New World' itself, in his case through the exciting environments of New York and Boston. It is not without reason that the *Symphony in E minor* was called 'from' and not 'about' the New World.

Once Dvořák's new symphony was finished, newspapers on both sides of the Atlantic Ocean reported on the remarkable contents of this work: the Bohemian had indeed composed a real American symphony. Dvořák himself did not shy from interviews in which he expanded on his acquaintance with spirituals. In *The New York Herald* he stated that he had found everything in Negro melodies that was 'needed for a great and noble music tradition'. A few days later this was also to be read in Paris and Prague. It was important news. The well-known composer Antonín Dvořák had indicated in so many words that the Americans, too, could finally measure up to the Bohemians, the Norwegians, the Finns and the Russians. It was exactly this that elicited such a negative response from his fellow composer Edward MacDowell.

In the first place, as MacDowell remarked with so much bitterness, this was no more than a Bohemian overcoat that Dvořák wanted to measure up for his students. Furthermore, 'Music that can be made by "recipe" is not music, but "tailoring".' In his eyes, this was just a trick. In this way, reasoned MacDowell, the Polish composer Moskowski could write Spanish dances, Cowen in England could create a Scandinavian symphony, the Norwegian Grieg Arabic music. 'And then we here in America have been offered a pattern for an "American" national musical costume by the Bohemian Dvořák.' The interesting thing about this re-action is that MacDowell apparently recognised no American influences in Dvořák's symphony, but mostly Bohemian ones. Dvořák was himself also in two minds about this. He might on one occasion say that the story of Hiawatha and the spirituals had given him ideas, and on another state that all of the melodies were entirely of his own invention, but that he had here and there tried to integrate into them the special qualities of the music of the Indians.

In essence, the discussion here is of course about the search for national identity. This might be Dvořák's own national identity or that of others, such as that of the African-American population or of the Indians, the original inhabitants of North America. Behind this lurks the question: what actually makes Bohemian music Bohemian, or American music American? Is there such a thing as a recognisable national identity, or is it, as MacDowell regarded it, all too often merely the result of an overcoat that you can put on quickly? A coat based on folk melodies, on scales, chords or rhythms that we recognise as belonging to a particular ethnic group or nation: as if we, after having heard that Max Bruch used a Jewish melody in his *Kol Nidrei*, were to casually label him as a Jewish composer. The use of the 18th-century melody of the *Kol Nidrei* is by no means exclusively reserved for Jews. We might just as well, on the grounds of the famous *Blue Rondo à la Turk* by Dave Brubeck, think that the use of a compound rhythm such as 2+2+2+3 or tá-da-tá-da-tá-da-tá-da-da, only occurs in Turkey, while there are also dances based on this rhythm in countries such as Bulgaria.

In fact, when listening to all kinds of music, we regularly ask ourselves if we can guess not only its geographical but also its historical origins, and in doing so we easily resort to all kinds of stereotypes. Everything which elsewhere in this book we have called the 'sound' of music could also be connected to the origins of that music. This is also exactly what MacDowell is warning us about, since the identity of a composer is not in the nature of the overcoat, but in the person who is wearing that overcoat. MacDowell even goes a substantial step further and states: 'before a people can find a musical writer to echo its genius it must first possess men who truly represent it – that is to say, men who, being part of the people, love the country for itself:

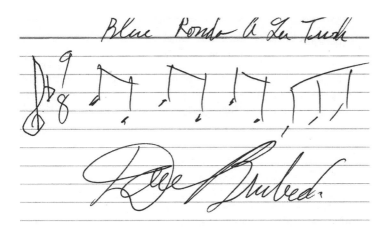

16. Dave Brubeck, *Blue Rondo à la Turk* with signature on an undated index card.

men who put into their music what the nation has put into its life.' In order to achieve this, Americans have to throw off the yoke of European hegemony and European cultural prejudices. They have to become themselves.

In this, we have to think about what Goethe wrote in 1789, the year of the French Revolution, in his essay *Einfache Nachahmung der Natur, Manier, Stil*: the thinking man 'finds a *tune* for himself, makes a *language* for himself in order to express anew and in his own way what touches his soul, [...] a language in which the spirit of the one who is speaking is brought into direct expression and given a meaning.' It is man himself who makes the language that suits his nature, a language with which he can express himself best, whether this is a language of words or one of musical notes. Goethe does not describe a direct link between a country and its culture, but does indicate one between the nature of a people (or individual) and their culture. In a sense this is the same thought as 'the bird is known by his note, a man by his word'. Goethe knew the writings of Plato and the relationship he had established between people and culture, between ethos and *mousike*.

The title of Goethe's essay, which can be translated as 'a simple imitation of nature, manner and style', can be linked to the concept of mimesis or imitation as this was represented in the ancient world by Plato and Aristotle (e.g. in relation to the harmony of the spheres), and subsequently conveyed first by the Romans and later by the Italian thinkers of the Renaissance as the basis for all art in the form of *imitatio della natura*. Thus music could represent an imitation of divine nature, of the nature of the cosmos, then of the nature of a language (every language), and finally of the nature of man, his character, his ratio. When we transfer this thought to people as a collective, to a folk or nation, we arrive at what MacDowell believed. Music represents the people that bring it forth by the nature of their folk or their country.

The rationale behind the vision which Goethe expressed in words, and which MacDowell acknowledged more than a century later, played an important role in the cultural development of the entire 19th century. The emergence of what as a rule are called 'national schools', the efforts of countries such as Norway, Russia, Finland and Denmark, but also Great Britain, Poland, Spain and Hungary to produce a recognisably distinctive culture, has everything to do with a search for identity. One might ask, why had this not happened before? Had the French, Italians, Spanish, the Germanic countries and the Austrians not had their own culture for a long time? Was there such a substantial difference between the development that occurred under the influence of nationalism and that of previous centuries?

The answer is both yes and no. If we take Goethe's words literally and concentrate on the 'own tune', then we are in fact looking for elements on the outskirts of culture, namely for recognisable melodies, rhythms and the like, in short for the 'Bohemian overcoat'. However, when we follow MacDowell's way and with it that of Plato, when we look for the character of a people, their national nature and 'soul', there wouldn't be any reason not to think of the music of Dufay as Northern French or Bourgondian, that of Cabezón as Spanish, Beethoven as Rhenish, or that of Byrd or Dowland as recognisably English. That Dufay also absorbed the influence of the English, the so-called 'contenance angloise' with its parallel thirds and sixths, or that Cabezón used variation techniques which we also encounter in the keyboard music of the Italians and the English of those times, or that Beethoven took on the influences of Haydn and Mozart as well as of Cherubini and Méhul, takes nothing away from the essence of their character, the impact of which is reflected in their music.

As is certainly the case in music, we are hardly used to peeling so many layers from an onion before we reach its central essence. Anyone who seeks to unearth the nature and origins of an artistic or cultural expression will have to remove all of the enveloping 'peel' which can be traced back to the 'outside world', such as the tunes and rhythms; in fact, everything which is hidden in that Bohemian overcoat. What remains can be described as the personal touch of the artist. Here we find his character, and we might recognise his connection with his country and his people. Here culture is the representation, the reflection of body and spirit, as was argued by the ancient Greeks. It is this that defines him from others, by the way in which only he interprets what has reached him from outside. Thus we come closer to his nature than to his culture. Once we see straight through all of the South German and Italian influences, through the influence of Johann Christian Bach and Joseph Haydn, the elements of elegant-aristocratic Rococo and sentimentally expressive Sturm und Drang, we will be able to recognise Mozart's own voice. On the basis of these thoughts, we will also recognise the works written by Dvořák in the United States as thoroughly Bohemian. He simply had no other overcoat than that of a Bohemian.

18. A memorable moment

Looking for some old documents one day, I found a reminiscence I had written at the end of the 1990s as the result of a remarkably moving moment on stage with the Residentie Orchestra in The Hague. This short story tells us something about the magic of the conductor. While composing may be mysterious to many, the art of conducting also has its secrets. What does that man or woman do in front of an orchestra? With their back to the audience? Sometimes the conductor waves ferociously with his arms, or communicates with the musicians with his entire body. At other moments we see absolutely nothing happening. It seems as though the many sounds we listeners experience coming from the stage are the result of a secret ritual. What, then, if the conductor were also just a child...

There he sits on the conductors' rostrum, in the maestro's place: a thin, tired-looking boy with big, dark eyes. He was rolled onto the stage in a wheelchair. He raises his hand gingerly. There is a moment of absolute silence, and then the orchestra starts Brahms's *Akademische Festouvertüre*. There is a brief eye contact between the boy and the musicians opposite him, but also amongst the musicians themselves. This is a new experience even for the most seasoned orchestral musician. Something remarkable is happening here. This boy, still a teenager, takes the orchestra through Brahms's score seemingly with the greatest of ease, like an experienced conductor: someone who doesn't have to think; someone who knows.

A few days earlier he had borrowed the score from the orchestra to study it with me in hospital, surrounded by nurses and apparatus. We go through it page after page, bar for bar, voice by voice and note by note. Sometimes he waves his hands above the sheets, as if for that brief moment a full orchestra is hidden in his room. Then he reads on in silence.

'It is a fine feeling, huh, when you can read a score, isn't it?' he sighs. In his mind he conducts the difficult transitions, the beautiful melodies, but all too soon he becomes tired and asks, eyes closed, for stories about conductors.

'How do you actually conduct? With your eyes open or closed?'

'Whatever you want,' I reply. 'Some conduct only with their eyes, others mainly with their hands.'

There are indeed great conductors who look as if they can't even beat the bars, while nothing goes wrong. They lead an orchestra through each score flawlessly, purely with their eyes, their knowledge of the notes and their driven musicality. The hands are merely a medium, and by no means always the most important.

The maestro of the Residentie Orchestra, the Russian Evgeni Svetlanov, even dared once to do this during a performance of Tchaikovsky's *Symphonie pathétique*. After only a few bars of the brilliant and swift third movement he completely stopped conducting, leading the orchestra only with his eyes. He missed nothing. Every entry was given with a single glance to the relevant musician. More was not necessary. He knew the score and the musicians knew their parts. The music took flight as if it was being invented on the spot, and transformed directly into sound as if by some magical power. This is the way that orchestras and conductors work the best. You simply forget them, and become surrounded purely by music.

Now here he sits, that skinny and seriously sick boy, weary but with a clear gaze before the orchestra, as if in a dream. How much depth, how much of a feeling for life can you put into this music? How many secrets can you reveal? He conducts like an experienced maestro. Not a single nuance escapes the economical gestures with which he leads the orchestra. Everyone on the stage can feel that this boy is entirely the master of this score: that he, child and adult, at the beginning of his life and at the same time close to its premature end, is able to elicit a wonderful world from Brahms's notes, something of which many an experienced conductor can only dream.

After the last note of Brahms's Festival Overture has sounded, the boy's teacher Jac van Steen takes over the reins, and the pressure is eased. Teacher and pupil exchange thoughts for a moment. After a few pointers, the difficult passages are run through once again. The woodwind should be more balanced, the strings a little brighter, and the phrasing is finished off. The music begins to speak, also to those who are not making music face to face with this young man, but who are viewing his small back from within the darkened hall.

The entire *Akademische Festouvertüre* sounds once again: festive, grand and intense. Sunlight and shadow compete for primacy. Seldom was a hymn so solemn and passionate. Then the exceptionally gifted young boy sinks against the back of his chair and closes his eyes. Van Steen thanks the orchestra. Everyone is impressed by the talent of this youth, and also by the knowledge that he is seriously ill. Conducting the Residentie Orchestra was his final wish.

Michel Bettenhaussen died six days later. He was sixteen years old. The memory of the gift of that remarkable moment remains in the memory of everyone who was present, a moment at which many were reminded all the more what feelings music can bring about, and made to realise anew why they chose this weighty and intense profession.

19. The conductor

Conductors have always been the subject of many stories, and not only because they are entitled to stand with their back to the audience. Orchestra members, reviewers and the public alike enjoy discussing their status and fortunes, their comings and goings. The number of anecdotes about conductors is as good as endless. More than any kind of musician in the 20th century, the conductor has become a symbol for stardom in music, a stardom that in the last fifty years has only been surpassed by that of pop artists. Of course, the status of the conductor as a star and an object of adoration by large groups of music lovers is by no means a new phenomenon. In the 18th century there was the same adoration for castrati, and in the 19th century for piano virtuosos such as Liszt, violin virtuosos like Paganini and singers such as Maria Malibran or Adelina Patti. In those days, the conductor as the subject of worship was still in the making.

Conducting in the form of beating the bars or giving the tempo is directly connected to the rise of performing music in groups, and in particular when each individual voice, previously sung or played by a single musician, began to be performed by increasing numbers, and moreover as soon as music increased in its complexity. The first conductors as givers of tempo and entries can be found in the 16th century. Tempo had previously been passed on using hand signals. The singers of a small choir could also lay their hand on the shoulder of the singer standing in front of them and synchronise the tactus (the beat) through a gentle squeeze. It is not clear whether the operas of Monteverdi, for example, were actually conducted, or whether the ensembles were led from the harpsichord or while playing the lute. Somebody must have kept everyone in line, sometimes by signals or ensuring the precision of an entry with the hand. In all probability this would have been the composer himself, who was almost always a member of the ensemble.

What we do know for certain is that the Italian dance master and composer Jean-Baptiste Lully acted very much as a conductor in his ballets and operas, usually with a roll of paper in his hand in order to make his indications more clearly visible. There is also the famous story of how he would beat time with a stick against the floor, and during a performance of his *Te Deum* struck his foot so hard that he ended up with a fatal infection. This tells us little about conducting in general and more about Lully's specific manner of conducting. Nowadays we can hardly imagine that a conductor would beat the bars for an orchestra with an audible tap. This was a common practice, however, even up until the first decades of the 19th century, although by then many conductors were waving with their bow or a roll of manuscript paper, and from 1830 also with a baton. The fact that the concertmaster was often equal in importance to the one who beat the bars can still be seen in the separate applause frequently given to the leader of the orchestra when he enters the stage ahead of the conductor, takes his place and gives the sign to start tuning up.

The fate of Lully is one of the few examples of conductors who have died *as a result of* exercising their profession. This is somewhat different to dying *during* the exercise of their profession, which is something that can happen to anyone, including conductors, including, for example, Eduard van Beinum, Dimitri Mitropoulos and Giuseppe Sinopoli and recently Israel Yinon. Even more striking were the deaths of Felix Mottl in 1911 and Joseph Keilberth in 1968. Both had a heart attack while conducting Wagner's *Tristan und Isolde* and died shortly afterwards. At least as legendary are the conductors who worked on beyond the moment that it was physically (and often as a result musically) still justifiable. Leopold Stokowski signed a recording contract for six years at the age of 94! This is not the place to list all of these venerably glorious and less glorious names, but the stories have given the profession of conductor a double reputation, namely that you can achieve great age and become very wealthy. Already in the 19th century conductors not infrequently earned twenty times as much as the musicians in their orchestras.

17. George Hayter, Carl Maria von Weber conducting *Der Freischütz* in Covent Garden Theatre, London, 1826. Weber is conducting here with a roll of paper in his hand (probably a sheet of manuscript paper).

The 'modern' conductor appeared on stage shortly after 1800. This shifted the leadership of a production from the 'primus inter pares', the first among equals – the concertmaster, the harpsichordist or pianist while sitting at his instrument – to that single person who stood imperiously in front of the orchestra and occupied himself almost exclusively with conducting. Louis Spohr, Carl Maria von Weber and Felix Mendelssohn were among the first specialist conductors. They rehearsed the orchestra, imposed their personal interpretations and had more and more to say about the final result. This was all the more noteworthy when they themselves had not composed the music. Thus Mendelssohn meant a great deal for the music of Berlioz, Wagner and Schumann. He chose the programmes for his orchestra in Leipzig, the famous Gewandhausorchester, and presented a multitude of young composers to its audiences.

Unlike many others of his time, Mendelssohn was aware of the amount of work needed to make an orchestra play properly, especially when the majority of orchestras still had many amateurs in their midst and didn't have the financial means to change this situation. While conducting once in Düsseldorf in 1833, he noted, as can be read in a letter to his friend Ignaz Moscheles, that each musician individually could play their notes correctly and rhythmically, but that the combined result was extremely out of tune and not at all together. A contemporary described Mendelssohn's behaviour on stage as fiery, precise and compelling. When he conducted, he was able to enthral everyone on the stage as well as in the hall through his baton. He sometimes led the orchestra with two hands, especially when he wanted to urge the musicians to play softly after a loud passage. Many reports of him project the impression of a conductor who always worked in the service of the music, and would as much as possible retreat as an individual. He was certainly not a showman or a virtuoso who yearned for public recognition. Before 1850 there was hardly a conductor who took his profession as seriously as Mendelssohn.

In 1869 Wagner published his essay *Über das Dirigieren* (On conducting), in which he first praises Mendelssohn for his professional competence, and then butchers him for being superficial and no more than a talented choirmaster. The title of Wagner's essay might lead us to conclude that it deals with the technique of conducting, but in reality Wagner analyses something which is essentially relevant to all musicians: the way in which the tempi and the phrasing in his own works and those of Mozart and Beethoven should be performed. Conductors in particular, who were by then the leading figures in public musical life, often got it entirely wrong. In his treatise Wagner pays a great deal of attention to what he describes as the intentions of his most important predecessors, Mozart and Beethoven, who in his eyes have their foundations in an important tradition of German art. *Kapellmeisters* are beating the bars, but great music has the right to deeply experienced and reliably truthful performances.

Unlike Wagner, Hector Berlioz had great admiration for Mendelssohn. He was also better placed than Wagner to compare him with others. In 1828, for instance, Berlioz was present at the first Parisian performance of Beethoven's *Fifth* by the newly-established orchestra of the Société des Concerts du Conservatoire, led by François-Antoine Habeneck. Beethoven's music had a huge impact on him, while the majority of the audience had trouble with the eccentricity and complexity of this symphony. Nine years later, the same Habeneck conducted Berlioz's *Requiem*, the *Grande Messe des morts*, in the Dôme des Invalides in Paris. No fewer than four hundred performers had been called up for this event, which was intended as a memorial concert for a General who had perished in the French colony of Algeria. The orchestra consisted of at least 180 musicians (including ten who played on sixteen kettle drums, and four brass ensembles) and there was a choir of well over two hundred singers. At the *moment suprême* in this score, in the *Tuba mirum*, when the drums and four brass groups enter with thunderous force, Habeneck decided to take a pinch of tobacco from his snuffbox. Berlioz, who noticed this just in time, could do little other than run forward to take over the conducting.

In 1855 in *L'art du chef d'orchestre,* Berlioz was also the first to analyse the practice technically. To begin with, he noted that there are few ill-natured conductors, but a great many who are completely incompetent.

> The conductor must *see* and *listen*, he must be *nimble* and *powerful*, he must *know* the composition, the *nature* and *range* of the instruments, he must be able to read the score and – apart from a special talent of which we will try to explain the constituent properties – possess other indefinable gifts without which an invisible connection between him and those he is leading cannot occur, and he will not be able to communicate his feelings to them, as a consequence of which the power, the supremacy, and the ability to give direction will slip away entirely.

18. J.J. Grandville, caricature of Hector Berlioz as a conductor, 1846.

A little further on, Berlioz clearly sets out how the conductor with his baton (which, he adds, should be a length of fifty centimetres) should beat the bar. For the first time, all of the details are explained with patience, professionalism and inventiveness. It would take another forty years or more before a study of comparable importance would appear: *Über das Dirigieren* (1896) by Felix Weingartner.

At events such as the performance of Berlioz's *Requiem,* it was absolutely necessary to have a conductor. Neither could the great symphonies by Beethoven or operas by composers such as Carl Maria von Weber be performed without professional leadership. We can also assume that in the second half of the 18th century even the mega-performances of Handel's *Messiah*, which often used hundreds of singers, would have been conducted. Indeed, the desire for large, larger, and largest as part of the new bourgeois pleasure in the arts had a direct effect on professional practice.

Several music educational institutions had already been established in the 17th century. In Italy these were given the name 'conservatorio', which meant that the pupils (the *conservati*) of this kind of institution were kept and cared for. Many of these institutions were therefore orphanages. In the second half of the 18th century, the name 'conservatoire' was connected with public music schools with a full-time day programme. The most famous and estimable example of these was the Conservatoire de musique in Paris, which arose in 1795 from the École nationale de musique, which in turn had been created from the École royale de chant and the École de musique municipale.

By around 1850 various European cities, including Paris, Prague, Vienna, London and Leipzig, possessed a conservatoire at which the most elementary principles of conducting could also be learned. A real professional training to become a conductor would have to wait, however, until the end of the 19th century. The bulk of conductors took up this profession in order to perform their own works. Thus, conducting composers played an important role on international concert stages until well into the 20th century, and conversely there were only few conductors who didn't also compose. Richard Wagner, Gustav Mahler, Richard Strauss, Igor Stravinsky, Leonard Bernstein and Pierre Boulez are good examples from the first category. Amongst the conductors who also composed we can name Wilhelm Furtwängler, Felix

Weingartner, Willem van Otterloo, Giuseppe Sinopoli and Esa-Pekka Salonen. In both categories, the reciprocity of proficiencies proved beneficial.

In general, almost every conductor has arrived at his profession from training as an instrumentalist, vocalist or composer. A number of conductors of name and fame didn't even gain their skills at a conservatoire, but learned by doing, through trial and error, by working as an assistant to experienced masters and by starting small, usually in the provinces, and with traditional methods of craftsmanship. The conductor Anton Seidl, who was world famous in the early 1900s, asserted that conducting was 'a gift of God'. In his eyes, training was hardly necessary: 'A talented person can learn the technique of the art in a few days. Someone without talent will never learn! People such as Von Bülow and Tausig just stood in front of the orchestra and conducted without having done any technical studies. They were gifted.' Although the situation in the past was no different from how it is now, the profession has become more complex, just like the music that has to be conducted.

The conductor's work is extremely versatile and demanding. Beating the bars is perhaps the smallest element, although it is certainly not unimportant for keeping everything together and giving the correct entries. Much more important is the development of a vision on the shape of a work, on its sound, on the balance of the instruments, and on convincing orchestral musicians and audiences of the intentions of the composer during rehearsals and in concert performance. For this, the conductor has to know the work thoroughly. As a teacher once told me: the score has to be in your head, and not your head in the score! Although it is not expected that a conductor should be able to play every instrument in the orchestra, he should know so much about them that he virtually can. He has to be able to work with the musicians as a craftsman, in a purely practical way. Even the most famous masters tend to forget that at times, and come up with all kinds of philosophical explanations, while the orchestral musician only wants to know: up or down bow, loud or soft, accented or non-accented. Orchestral musicians only really give themselves completely to a conductor when he is entirely master of all his materials and no one in the orchestra is thinking, 'I could do that too...'

It is not entirely without reason that an orchestral musician is sometimes of the opinion that the conductor is only getting in the way, and not contributing to the honour and glory of the music. Bearing in mind that an orchestra consists of highly qualified professionals, the conductor needs to be supremely capable in order to prevail naturally without being a bully. A few of the most famous conductors, such as Mahler and Toscanini, behaved as genuine tyrants, but the social hierarchies were different then. Even so, the desire to be swept along in the adventure of music has remained undiminished for the orchestral musician. On the basis of his professional competence and great passion, the conductor must therefore be capable of making the musicians true participants in the project we call a concert, so that the final result will be a genuine collaboration. This certainly demands knowledge, experience and craftsmanship, but also charisma.

In the end, that last qualification, that charisma, is possibly the most important. It distinguishes the ordinary practitioner from the outstanding conductor. Many stories are told about this magical quality; for example, about the moment that the Berlin Philharmonic was rehearsing and as if by a miracle, the sound changed. The timpanist in the orchestra saw the old principal conductor, Wilhelm Furtwängler, standing in the back of the hall. Merely his presence was enough.

Indeed, when we now look back on some two centuries of renowned orchestral conductors, it is mostly the charismatic figures that are remembered: the tyrants, the autocrats and the aristocrats. Others undoubtedly knew their trade to the last detail, and performed their duties with great integrity, but apparently more is required to become a legend. Richard Wagner was such a legendary figure. By his twenties he had already conducted in many theatres, and knew the business of the orchestra pit and the stage as few others. He was in control of everything. Contemporary reports relate that Wagner didn't beat the bars in a conventional way; sometimes his hands would even stop moving entirely, in order to then lead the orchestra to a climax. He played the orchestra like an instrument.

At the end of the 19th century Wagner's disciple and assistant, Anton Seidl, wrote a short undated essay about the conducting of his master:

> Upon all who heard or played under him he exerted an ineradicable influence. His music, frequently rugged in contrasts and daring leaps, is also insinuating and suave at times, and so, too, was his conducting: one moment he would be high in air, the next crouched under his desk; one moment he would menace the bass drummer, and the next flatter the flutist; now he would draw long threads of sound out of the violinists, and anon lunge through the air at the double basses, or with some daring remark help the violoncellists to draw a *cantilena* full of love-longing out of their thick-bellied instruments. His musicians feared him and his demoniac, sarcastic face, and wriggled to escape unscathed from his talons.

Comparable stories can be read about Mahler, and to a lesser extent about Hans von Bülow, Hanns Richter, Hermann Levi, Arthur Nikisch or Richard Strauss. Incidentally, Nikisch was one of the first to conduct from memory. Arturo Toscanini, one of the genuine greats of the first half of the 20th century, was notorious for his sarcastic and sharp-tongued remarks. In his case, this did not come about as a show of strength, but from purism, from the search for the perfect idea in music. Rudolf Escher wrote an essay on this, *Toscanini en Debussy, magie der werkelijkheid* (*Toscanini and Debussy, the magic of reality*). Toscanini was a perfectionist who doubted himself and his capacity to achieve that perfection, but he was also a hothead who could afford his eruptions of temper in a time that the hierarchies of power were still sharply defined.

What these conductors – autocrats, aristocrats or purists – had in common and what sets them apart from most of today's major conductors is that they gave more than half of their time to contemporary music. Mendelssohn, Berlioz, Wagner, Mahler, Bülow, Richter, Levi, Nikisch, Strauss, Toscanini, Mengelberg and others of their generation of course conducted the music of Mozart (certain works a great deal), Haydn (a little), Beethoven (very regularly), Weber, Mendelssohn and Schumann (sometimes) or Bach (at most when arranged for orchestra). However, they owed their fame to presenting the music of their own time: for example, much Wagner and Brahms, Tchaikovsky and Strauss, later also Debussy, and numerous other contemporaries who are hardly known today. In addition, the composers amongst the conductors also brought their own music into the limelight.

After the First World War and even more so after the Second World War, symphony orchestras became repositories for mainly classical-romantic repertoire. Contemporary music was then and still is all too infrequently heard, but that is another story. This reduction in the repertoire made it necessary to engage specialist conductors who had a command of contemporary music with all of its highly complex rhythms, time signatures or fluctuations in tempo. These conductors also understood the sign language required: for example, counting with the fingers or the indication of the division of time with the arms as pointers around an imaginary clock.

At almost the same time, another type of conductor moved forward: the specialist in the performance techniques of the 18th and early 19th centuries. The first group mostly consisted of technically highly skilled and schooled conductors (initially often the composers of the new scores themselves) and the second group of performing musicians of 'early music', who gradually became conductors through leading their own ensembles. Since the last generation, these various specialisms have now become a part of the training of every young conductor.

There are actually no criteria for determining whether a conductor may or may not be needed. Although a large symphony orchestra without a conductor is extremely rare (such as the Persimfans Orchestra in the Soviet Union in the 1920s), some orchestras have worked regularly without a conductor. In these cases, the concertmaster then takes over some of the leadership duties. With chamber orchestras and small ensembles, the presence of a conductor is more a matter of convenience than of strict necessity.

These days a conductor is at one moment the director of a complex operating company of musical specialists, at another the project leader of a small team. With chamber orchestras, it can very well be the concertmaster or one of the other musicians who takes the lead. But in the best cases, a conductor can streamline and speed up the rehearsal process because he has a complete overview of the entirety of a score. A conductor can at times oversee more than forty parts, from the piccolo at the top of the score to the double bass at the bottom. No orchestral musician is capable of this while performing, if only since it would be physically impossible to turn the pages of a large score every few bars and still be able to play an instrument.

The conductor also finds himself in a convenient place, in the middle and in front of the orchestra, a place from which the balance between the many instruments can be heard well. It seems so obvious, but we often forget that the flautist or the horn player or the violinist at the rear of the second violins, or the double bassist at the upper right of the stage, cannot possibly judge how his instrument fits within the entirety of the intended sounds. When there is no conductor, experienced orchestra members can go a long way with their eyes and ears, certainly when the various instruments don't have to go their own way too often and everything can be kept more or less together by ear alone. Creating a good balance does, however, require an ear at a distance.

There is something else which makes a conductor indispensable. Our music practice during the last century has been less and less focused on first performances; on becoming acquainted with new pieces. Instead, we listen mainly and by preference to striking and newly experienced performances of well-known repertoire, of the great masterpieces. Now, in principle all of the exceptional and surprising insights of a piece of music are to be found somewhere in the score. Because we can and want to hear the same works hundreds of times, there must be something each time that grabs and holds us. This is what Wagner was referring to in 1869, and to which Mahler, Toscanini, Mengelberg, Furtwängler, Von Karajan, Celibidache and every great conductor of today owes their name and fame: their remarkable and often exceptional interpretations. That became their trademark in the 20th century. Both the musicians on stage and the music lovers in the hall crave special experiences. The spark has to be there if we want to be able to address and liberate our emotions, and to experience that moment of sublimation. For that we have to thank the great conductors and all of the musicians who are able to do this.

20. The performing artist

One night I was driving through the country with the elderly master Olivier Messiaen. We passed the time with small talk and conversation about music, as well as about his many journeys, from Japan to the national parks in Utah in the United States. I asked him why he spent his precious time on these numerous travels, which were often not intended for notating the singing of unknown birds or to gain inspiration for new compositions, but purely and simply to be present at concerts of his music. These were rarely even premieres, which would have justified such journeys, however far. He would travel all this distance for yet another performance of the *Turangalîla Symfonie* or the *Quatuor pour la fin du temps*. In my eyes, this was lost time and energy for someone who already composed painfully slowly, and from whom we would have much appreciated some new works.

In all its clarity and honesty, Messiaen's answer was also cheerfully childlike:

> You should go to as many performances of your own music as possible. That is good for the contact with the musicians who play your music. And don't forget, young friend, that you must always be intensely satisfied with the achievements of the musicians. Never complain, never be disappointed. Compliment the musicians, praise them to the heavens. You need them! If you are nice to them then they will be nice to you, and will perform your music again and again.

But what is to be done with criticism; with unfulfilled wishes? Messiaen was convinced that you should treat musicians with a soft hand and with much respect. They are of no value to you if they no longer want to be committed to your music, just because you are grumpy and cross. Indeed, you need them.

Perhaps this is the most important difference between a painter or sculptor and a composer, between a poet or playwright and a composer, or even between a jeweller or cabinetmaker and a composer. The composer, just like the choreographer, needs someone who translates the work of art into real sounds or movements in order to make it understood. At a glance, a painting, sculpture, poem, script, jewel or chair is entirely in and of itself. What you see is present in a concrete sense, what you read are words with a concrete meaning. Even when you then have to look behind those images or read between the lines of the poem, even when actors and directors make their own interpretation of a text, the initial superficial confrontation already delivers a tangible result. Music and dance do not have this quality, and music even less so than dance, since it is not even physically present in its manifest form, even though we as listeners can respond to it in a physical way. The presentation of music is merely vibrating air, usually turned into sound by means of symbols on a sheet of paper.

There are of course always composers who perform their own music. These include artists such as Bernard de Ventadorn, Niccolò Paganini or Frédéric Chopin, but also numerous *chansonniers* and modern troubadours, singer-songwriters, pop and jazz musicians who basically need no one but themselves in order to convert their musical thoughts into sound. Even then, however, they are different people as performers of their own music than when they are its composer, whether or not they play from sheet music, from memory or while improvising. When even just one single other musician ventures to perform the composer's music, he will have to make a translation. Since every performing musician has to form his own image of the music in the first place on the basis of the score – from that sheet with its symbols, which are a mystery to so many – and furthermore, if possible, from underlying ideas, background information and the like, all of this together provides a second translation.

Curiously, it turns out that this second translation has become the core of musical practice in our Western culture. After all, since we started to preserve music in writing, we have created the possibility of it being used by others. This has even become one of the pillars of the modern music industry: the performance of the works of another, the interpretation of the thoughts of another. Most contemporary musicians know no better and are often capable of nothing other than performing covers, the notes written by someone else. We don't have to be condescending about this, since many scores demand a high degree of specialisation on the part of their performers. The downside, however, is that only a few musicians can execute their craft with the experience and knowledge of a composer. Over more than a century, the gap has grown larger than ever before.

Moreover, until well into the 19th century mostly new works were being performed, music of which the ink of the manuscript or printed edition was still wet. In musical terms, looking backwards hardly existed. Only in exceptional cases were compositions performed more frequently than for the one occasion for which they had been written, usually as a request or a commission. Repetition could be the result of recycling (evidently a successful piece of music can be used again, with different words, in a different context or set for different instruments), or simply due to great popularity. Over the centuries handwritten copies of much-loved works were widely circulated and emerged in many countries. The music of Josquin des Prez, for instance, or Monteverdi, Purcell, Haydn and Beethoven, crossed many borders in their lifetimes. Not long after they were released, the scores of Haydn and Beethoven even appeared on music stands in North America.

But even in cases of exceptional popularity, the chance was quite small that a listener could make comparisons of quality by hearing two performances of the same work by different musicians in quick succession. Only when, on the one hand, our concert podium increasingly began to look like a museum for old and proven art (processions of musicians passing by, all playing the same works), and on the other hand, the means of capturing and reproducing sound, and thus of the performances of pieces of music became possible (with dozens of recordings of Beethoven's *Fifth* as a consequence), only then did musicians increasingly start to compete with each other in their performances of the same works. Now we use more words to discuss the differences between performances than to analyse a performance as an independent phenomenon, or to scrutinise the composition that is being played and place it in an interesting context.

Nowadays a musician has to measure himself on multiple fronts against his colleagues, and not infrequently even against himself: firstly in the here and now (Murray Perahia against Maria João Pires), then from the present to the past (Murray Perahia against Wilhelm Kempf in the 1950s, or Dinu Lipatti in the 1940s or even Rachmaninoff in the 1930s – the living competing with the dead), then relative to himself (Murray Perahia in the concert hall against his own CD recordings or even various versions by him of the same work on CD), and finally, still within the discipline but from various historical perspectives (Murray Perahia on a modern concert grand piano against Ronald Brautigam on a copy of a fortepiano from the time of Mozart or Beethoven).

The first category of confrontations is inherent in the profession. For many centuries, performing musicians have been vying with each other for the honour of being considered the best on their instrument. There are many reports of competitions between singers, pianists or violinists. This often involves both the compositional mastery of the craft (playing variations on a given theme on the spot) and technical mastery (who can play the fastest or in the most refined way, or who can perform the most surprising tricks): whether it is about Apollo and Marsyas, who tried to outdo each other (there was always a significant role for music and singing during sports events in ancient Greece at Delphi, as well as at later Olympic Games in the early 20th century); or about Mozart, who went into competition against

Clementi in 1781 with the Emperor Joseph II and the Russian Grand Duke Paul as the jury; or about the many young musicians in competitions all over the world who go on stage to measure themselves irrevocably against their peers. And if the musicians don't do it themselves, the public and critics certainly will. These days we can hardly judge anything without comparing it to something else.

The second and third confrontations are the direct result of technical achievements in the last 125 years. Not only has technology given us the possibility to reproduce a work of art in such quantities that more people than ever before can become acquainted with and use it, but through the recording on film of musicians, dancers and actors, we are actually able to analyse, copy and imitate their way of performing, and finally the earlier presentation becomes an object which can entirely in and of itself be compared with the same object of today. This is true as long as technology doesn't stand in our way, for a scratchy mono recording from the 1920s will of course hardly stand up to a modern recording. The majority of people would therefore not choose Willem Mengelberg with the Concertgebouw Orchestra playing Mahler's *Fourth Symphony* over Bernard Haitink with the same orchestra playing the same work, recorded half a century later. After all, it is not easy to listen to a poor-quality recording, certainly when the beauty of the sound wins over the content of the interpretation or the quality of a composition.

Those who are not bothered by such things will, for instance, notice that Artur Schnabel in his historic cycle of the complete Beethoven sonatas from 1935 is indeed strong competition for Alfred Brendel, who has recorded the entire cycle no fewer than three times (around 1960, then in the 1970s and one last time in the 1990s). In this way Brendel competed with himself, and perhaps not unintentionally. The cycle from the 1990s has the purpose of showing us that Brendel continued to develop his playing, and that his insights with regard to Beethoven were not set in stone. How many conductors these days are not compared in their performances with the recordings of the same works that were made between 1950 and 1980 by Herbert von Karajan and 'his' Berlin Philharmonic? And Von Karajan, who released numerous records and CDs of Beethoven's nine symphonies, also competed with himself.

The extent to which a performing musician can be his own competitor is quite manifest when during a live performance he has to fight against his own interpretations on record or CD. In 1974, Alfred Brendel gave one of his legendary recitals in the Concertgebouw in Amsterdam. The venue was sold out. There were more people in the hall than would be acceptable to the Fire Department today: some 2,300 listeners, right up to a small ring of seats around the piano on the stage. I had brought along a student friend, who expressed his adoration for Brendel via a few gramophone records that he regularly had blaring at high volume through his dorm room. Now we were sitting in the middle of the front balcony, the maestro directly in front of us on stage. When the recital was over, and after the applause and cries of bravo had coerced one encore after another, I asked inquisitively, 'And? How did you like it?' 'Well,' said my friend, 'it was beautiful, yes, really, but I still think the record at home is much more beautiful.' 'But this was living music, played by a living person especially for us here in the concert hall.' 'That may be true,' was his laconic reply, 'but I still prefer the record, without an audience, without the restless disturbance of a musician on the stage, just at home in my own room, where because of that recording nothing can go wrong with that performance.'

That 'canned' performance – whether it reaches us by way of a record, CD, the radio or the Internet, whether it has been put together with a great deal of editing (comparable with Photoshop, but with sound) or recorded live during a concert – has made attending a concert hall unnecessary for many people. At the same time, this technology has brought millions of people closer to music and to musicians. This is the strength of recording, and at the same time its danger, since the musician of whom a recording is made is not the same as the one playing in a concert venue. The performance on the CD is not that of the concert hall. Sound recordings create a different, new reality. Microphones alter the dynamic framework. Everything seems closer, and often *is* closer. The balance and depth of a recording are not the same as those in a concert hall. While the performance itself is already a coloured representation of the idea of a composition, the recording of that same performance is a knowingly manipulated representation of a representation.

Next there is the fourth form of competition, one that has certainly played a more significant role since the Second World War: the degree of authenticity of a performance, particularly when this refers to 'early' music. This is actually a separate story, but still worth considering in this context. As music of bygone eras became an increasing part of contemporary concert practice – a frequently referred-to historic moment for this is the first modern, which is to say 19th-century performance of Bach's *St Matthew Passion* in 1829 – more attention was given, especially after the First World War, to the original versions or editions of music from before 1800, the so-called 'Urtext editions'. However, most music of the 17th and 18th centuries was still performed on modern instruments, with a few exceptions such as the harpsichordist Wanda Landowska, the violist Paul Hindemith (who also played the viola d'amore), and the recorder players Arnold and Carl Dolmetsch. This changed dramatically after the Second World War with the pioneering work of the harpsichordist Gustav Leonhardt, the recorder player Frans Brüggen, the gambist Nikolaus Harnoncourt and many other advocates of an authentic sound in early music.

When a keyboard work by Bach is played on a concert grand piano, we can safely assume that a translation has taken place, also at the level of the choice of instrument. Although a forerunner of the piano existed in Bach's time, we can be reasonably sure that Bach would not have had such an instrument in mind, or considered using it. This is not to say that this is not permitted. That Bach wrote for a harpsichord and Mozart for an orchestra with probably no more than twenty musicians doesn't mean that they didn't dream of other possibilities. The symbols in a score do not only encode the contents of probable performances, but also a large number of unlikely ones. We cannot therefore ignore the unlikely, even though the likely performances will be closer to the sound perception of the composer.

The choice of instruments has direct consequences for the sound of a performance, and thus for the nature of the translation made by the musician from score to sound, but the ways of playing that chosen instrument are also decisive for the sound. One of the most noticeable characteristics is that of vibrato. Associated with this is the central question: should there be vibrato when playing a wind or string instrument or when singing? After all, vibrato is not a built-in mechanism, but a learned technique that can be switched on and off. We also know that vibrato was principally seen as decoration until well into the 19th century; as an addition to be used along with other techniques of ornamentation, for instance in the case of long held notes.

There is yet another follow-up question in this regard: in the 16th century, for example, would there have been a demonstrable difference between singing in Italy, in Spain, in England or in Central Europe? If this were the case, should this be taken into account when we perform the vocal works of Palestrina or Monteverdi, Cristobal de Morales or Tomás Luis de Victoria, Thomas Tallis or Thomas Weelkes, Hans Leo Hassler or Heinrich Schütz? At that time, musicians were sensitive to anything that could adversely affect the exact pitch and purity of a note. In solo parts a light shaking was indeed appreciated as an ornament, a 'vox humana' or 'vox tremula'. In around 1620 Praetorius translated the term 'vox tremula' from wind instruments to the human voice as a 'bebende Stimme'; in other words, performed with a quiver, something that is different to vibrato. The 'bebende Stimme' is particularly nimble, has a sweet and tender sound, can sing 'smooth' or straight notes and is in possession of a good breathing technique: a voice with life in it. In Italian, English and Spanish sources, an equal emphasis is given to the clear pronunciation of words and a precise rhythmic diction.

Only in the second half of the 19th century did vibrato become a part of the sound of all instruments (including the voice) to which it could be applied. This vibrato, sometimes fast and heavy, sometimes slow or mild, has also become a personal signature *par excellence* for a musician, and therefore a characteristic of musical beauty. Whether or not to use vibrato remains a serious point of discussion, just like the sliding from one note to another, the *portamento*. In the course of the 20th century, people began to question the tastefulness of this technique. Before, however, it was an obvious way to move the hand from one position to another, for instance on a violin. Thus, if we pursue an authentic performance of Tchaikovsky's *Violin Concerto*, then the first entry of the soloist should begin with a *portamento*, tasteless or not.

And what about the bassoon solo at the beginning of Stravinsky's *Le sacre du printemps*? Even for a player of the lighter French 'basson', this solo would have been a breakneck stunt in 1913. Part of the feeling of a primal force immediately at the beginning of the *Sacre* is in the authenticity of its performance. Nowadays this same solo is almost a piece of cake for any bassoonist; at least, that's the way the music sounds: sweet, song-like and smooth. Gone is the primal power...

By way of conclusion we can state that our musical culture would be unimaginable without the various links between the arts of creating, performing and listening or evaluating. A relatively small number of composers (though still tens of thousands worldwide) have written for many times more performing musicians (several hundreds of thousands), to reach and satisfy a now massive public (in our times, more people than have ever listen to music: many tens of millions). Composers cannot do without performing musicians, but in turn these performing musicians cannot do without the composers. Without the latter, there would be nothing to perform. The audience, however, needs both, as do both of them need their audience. The written score has to sound in order to exist. The performing musician must therefore play to give the music its right to existence and to breathe life into it, and the listener must listen in order to absorb the music into his existence, his thoughts and feelings; in order to confirm it as a work of art and therefore allow it to become part of a collective culture.

19. The author with Olivier Messiaen, 1986 (photo © Co Broerse).

Part E

21. Lully: the King is dancing

In his memoires, Louis XIV wrote, 'all of our citizens are generally delighted to see that we like what they like or in which they best succeed. In this way we have a hold on their spirit and their heart, and occasionally many times to a much greater extent than through payments or good deeds.' In this he was referring to dance. Louis loved dance passionately, as did his entourage. With the statement quoted, the King indicated that dance served a dual purpose: he demonstrated that he was both a master of dance as well as that of his subjects. Dancing was directly connected to the status of the King.

Louis XIV started to dance as a child and practised the art for almost a quarter of a century, with daily exercises and participation in numerous performances. In 1725 Pierre Rameau wrote of him in *Le Maître à danser* that his preferred form of dance was the noble and serious Courante:

> Verily he danced this better than anyone else at Court, and endowed her an infinite grace. But what provides even more proof for the kinship and penchant that His Majesty has for dance is the fact that this great Conqueror, despite the hard work which has always kept him occupied, for more than twenty to twenty-two years has never deprived Monsieur de Beauchamps of the honour of guiding him for those few hours in this noble exercise.

He would dance, however busy his work schedule. In the newspaper of 8th January 1663, it was printed that 'the King, exhausted by the efforts with which His Majesty tirelessly works for the welfare of his subjects, enjoyed distraction in the Cardinal's palace by [dancing in] a ballet with seven acts, entitled the *Ballet des Arts*.'

Dancing was part of the education of a nobleman. In 1528 the Mantovanian writer Baldassare Castiglioni had written in his 'handbook for the courtier', *Il libro del cortegiano*, that a nobleman must learn mastery of the sword and the spear, and in particular also music, rhetoric and dance. This should enable a nobleman to maintain a beautiful lady satisfactorily. In 1641 Monsieur de Saint-Hubert published a tract on the *ballets de cour*, in which he remarked: 'Everyone knows that in order to finish a young nobleman it is important that he can ride a horse, can shoot weapons and can dance. The first contributes something to his skills, the second to his courage, and the last to the elegance of his posture.' Dance was not only an expression of art and culture, but also as training for the soldier. In the patent for the Académie royale de danse, Louis wrote in 1661: 'It is one of the most valuable and useful art forms for nobles and others who have the honour to be in our presence, not only in our armies in times of war, but also in our ballets in times of peace.'

Historically, there had always been much dancing in the French Court, some of it compulsory (Louis's father had done it much against his will). An extra element was soon added to dancing through the development of the *ballet de cour*, in which dance and allegory were brought together in order to mark important political moments. Louis XIV had been brought up in this tradition, but because he was an avid dancer he didn't want to stay on the sidelines. Influenced by his mentor, Cardinal and First Minister Mazarin, he let himself be schooled by his dance masters to the extent that he ultimately reached the same standard as the professionals. In fact, he would have preferred to surpass them. Louis emphatically differentiated himself as a dancer from his subjects by not merely doing what they also did, but by doing it better, and always in roles which clearly showcased his 'divine' position.

An important aspect in all of this – in the thinking of Mazarin, the King and indeed the entire aristocracy, and not only in France – was the symbolism of the chosen themes or subjects, the libretti. Ancient culture had come to attention during the Renaissance, and in particular the Greek tragedies and the mythological and epic stories received much acknowledgement and recognition from the nobility. Had they no desire to go through life as gods and heroes, or at least to be considered as such? From the start, both opera and ballet were dominated by precursors from the ancient world. Dance and music blended very well with the old tragedies. Louis XIV selected his dance roles carefully so that he could depict exactly those mythical characters that suited his status as a person, as royalty, indeed as a divine figure.

There was a sophisticated strategy behind all of this, tightly directed by Mazarin from the outset. How to turn a barely four-year-old King into a powerful sovereign, and that in a time of sustained political chaos? Mazarin decided to make symbolism and reality reinforce each other. Louis's second name was Dieudonné, or 'given by God', for good reason. This divine status had to lead to a symbol of absolute power, and since the King clearly had a great talent for dancing, Mazarin saw the advantages of emphasising that particular element within the culture of the French Court, to see it elevated and in particular personified. Where dancing had originally been a companionable amusement, an elegant pastime that suited the nobility with an occasional allegorical dance as a political signal, Mazarin decided to turn Louis XIV into a dancer beyond compare. The King not only took part in courtly dances in the halls of the palace, but also went on stage. Dance was elevated into a highly personal means of displaying the King to the Court and beyond.

Louis appeared in an official ballet for the first time at the age of twelve, *Le ballet de Cassandre*. His most notable and symbolic role was two years later, in 1653: that of the god of light, the sun, and wisdom, as Apollo in the appearance of 'Le soleil levant', the rising sun in the *Ballet de la Nuit*. The music for this was largely composed by Jean de Cambefort, Michel Lambert and Louis de Mollier on a libretto by Isaac de Benserade. Louis XIV, then aged fourteen, danced as many as six different roles, something he would do frequently in many later ballets. It was with this ballet that Louis established his name as the 'Sun King'. Next to the professional Court dancers there were two young dance masters alongside him in the *Ballet de la Nuit*: Pierre Beauchamps and

20. Henri de Gissey, costume for Louis XIV as Apollo in the *Ballet royal de la Nuit*, 1653.

Giovanni-Battista Lulli, better known as Jean-Baptiste Lully. Beauchamps had already worked with the King for some years, teaching him the moves and positions. Lully made his debut as a dancer at the court in the *Ballet de la Nuit* alongside the King. The event provided the King with his new title and in the same year, the position of Compositeur de la musique instrumentale du roi for Lully. To acquire this title Lully may also have composed some dances for the *Ballet de la Nuit*, but any evidence to substantiate this is now lost.

From 1653 onwards a royal ballet was performed every year in the carnival period, amounting to 27 in total. Several times, the King appeared in these in the role of 'the Sun'. The newly appointed court composer Lully provided the music for some of the most important royal ballets, including the *Ballet royal d'Alcidiane* (1658), the *Ballet royal de l'impatience* (1661), the *Ballet royal de la Naissance de Vénus* (1665) and the *Ballet royal de Flore* (1669). However, none of these was as extensive as the *Ballet de la Nuit*, which of course served an exceptional purpose. In this production, more than forty different dances and entrances followed each other, divided over three acts which each lasted three symbolic hours. The guests were entertained in the great hall of the Hôtel de Bourbon, also known as Le Petit-Bourbon, with more than twelve hours of music, dance, spoken word and festive banquets. One of the visitors complained that he had to wait outside for more than three hours before being admitted. The performance lasted from six o'clock in the evening to six the next morning, at the appearance of the sun, both literally and figuratively, in the person of the King. After the first performance, the *Ballet de la Nuit* was repeated six times, and always to a packed house.

'The King's costume was richly covered with gold stitching and a multitude of rubies and the rays around his head were made of diamonds. The crown on his headdress was made with rubies and pearls and elaborated with many red and white feathers.' This was how Louis XIV was presented in the figure of Apollo as a symbol of his kingship. Members of the highest nobility were required to perform as guest dancers, and showed their loyalty to the King as part of the ballet. Even the Duke of York, later to be King James II of England, took part in the dance. The second wife of Louis XIV, Madame de Maintenon, later remarked that the severity of the rules at a monastery was nothing compared with the rules of etiquette to which the courtiers of the King were subjected. The surviving choreographies of the ballets stand as witness to this.

A year later the King performed in an Italian ballet comedy by Francesco Buti, *Les noces de Pélée et Thétis*, translated into French by De Benserade and with music by Carlo Caproli, reportedly in front of more than thirty thousand people in total. The first performance on 14th April 1654 was attended by Charles II of England (the father of the Duke of York), who had fled to France from Cromwell. This was followed by three performances a week until the end of May. It was commissioned by none other than Mazarin. Almost the entire cast of the *Ballet de la Nuit* was present once again, and again the King appeared on stage as Apollo and also danced another five roles. Thus, Mazarin and Louis XIV fulfilled their aim that within a few years the King, by dancing, should become a symbol for everything a modern autocratic monarch should be. Louis and his successors would remain absolute rulers until the French Revolution in 1789, the same year in which the Académie royale de danse, the first professional dance school established by Louis XIV in 1661, was closed down: dance and power going hand in hand.

As an Italian in France, Cardinal Mazarin must have been well aware that in the patronage of the arts, he had a spiritual weapon that could be used in Machiavellian ways in order to win and retain power both for himself and the young King. He was not exclusively interested in dance. Until his death in 1661, when Louis took every power for himself, Mazarin played a substantial role in the development of the sovereign's tastes, for instance by promoting the establishment of the Académie des Beaux-Arts and by putting forward his countryman Lully as a dancer, and especially as a composer. He ensured that the visual arts, literature and music became an integral part of the Court, thereby allowing him to impose his opinion of what the image of the Court should be to the outside world, and how the King should be regarded by his citizens. Mazarin also divided the entirety of French culture into institutes that were governed by artists specially appointed by him, who with absolute power over their domains were able to reign in much the same way as did the King himself over his country and his subjects.

Thus we see that within a decade, music in France fell entirely under the omnipotence of Jean-Baptiste Lully, and with it, the musical rules which he developed. The French overture is the best example of this. From the overtures for the early French *ballets de cour*, with their formal but also rather dull march-like rhythms, Lully single-handedly created a musical prologue which was festive, sharply tailored and filled with contrasts. In this he may have been inspired by the 'entrees' that had already been written for Louis XIII, or by the forceful overture which De Cambefort had composed for the *Ballet de la Nuit*. With strongly marked rhythms and a driving pulse, both the power and the elegance of French courtly culture were reflected. Lully's overtures swiftly began to lead a life of their own, freed from the chain of dances that they were intended to precede. As the first movement of a suite of dances, as opening for an opera or even a religious work, these overtures became symbolic of French style.

Nowadays we would call Lully a style icon. He came to France as a young man and learned by experience. Although he was pushed forward as a result of his Italian origins by Mazarin (who until his death continued to sign official documents either with his French name or the original Italian, Mazarini), Lully preferred to see himself as a Frenchman. It is not inconceivable that it was this desire that caused him to be more Catholic than the Pope. He had made his mark on French music even before being given French nationality in 1662. The arrival in Paris of Francesco Cavalli in that period brought Lully into competition with the Italian grand master, and in every imaginable terrain he did this through music that was perceived as typically French by his contemporaries.

Lully may have begun his career as a dancer and as a composer for dances, but as soon as he had the opportunity, he showed a preference for composing music for the theatre (in comedies by Molière and with operas) and religious works for the Court Chapel. His ambition was to gain leadership over the King's orchestra, Les 24 Violons du Roi. Lully's ballets, the operas and the *grands motets* were found to meet the highest demands of the King. Never before had French music blossomed to such an extent, and with such an international appeal. Lully's music soon became popular in England and the Germanic countries. Together with his first minister Mazarin, Louis XIV must have acknowledged at an early stage that it was Lully who was capable of developing a musical style which would honour the King, which would serve as an example of what French state music (as this is how we could see the new music) should be, and which suited the new palace in Versailles, which was brought into use in 1682 and thereby became the powerful political and cultural centre of France. Lully was considered the highest authority and his music as a model for composers until well into the 18th century.

Throughout all of this, was Louis XIV an entirely altruistic supporter of music, theatre and dance? The King invested his wealth and that of his subjects in building what was then the largest palace in Europe, with the most magnificent gardens, and held the most sumptuous events in his palace and in these gardens. Louis XIV employed the composer Lully, the playwright Molière, the landscape architect André Le Nôtre and the painter Charles Le Brun, and established the Académie royale de danse, the Comédie Française and the Académie royale de musique, and left his mark on art and culture throughout the entire country. Naturally, he was in no way disinterested. In the same way that he presented himself as a divine dancer, Louis saw all of art that he financed as having concrete aims. Everything has its price. This was simply a matter of commercial exchange.

Art represents its patron; therefore all of the art that was created at the request of King Louis had to have royal allure.

The King went so far in this that he not only brought numerous institutes to life, but also set out rules for truly royal art. Anyone who refused to follow these rules stood a good chance of being expelled and having their royal privileges withdrawn. In 1683 Louis even organised a competition for a 'sous-maître' for the royal chapel, in order to have the opportunity of dismissing lesser talents at his Court in exchange for better musicians. Thirty-five composers in the service of the French dioceses were summoned to the Court to present a motet that would be performed in front of the King. The best fifteen composers were then locked into a room and made to write a new motet on the text of Psalm 32 (*Beati quorum*). A position at the Court Chapel lay in the offing for the four best composers. The choice of the King was decisive, with Lully by his side.

Church, Court and State do not support art purely for art's sake. It is for the display of themselves, as Prelate, King, Head of State, Government. Patronage is a demonstration of power and provides the patron with an identity. Meaningful support for the arts will therefore only occur when the patron believes he will benefit, or if he considers that his subjects will benefit, since then he will ultimately also see the benefit of this in turn. Support for the arts is therefore a business transaction, even when a more ideological position is taken as its aim. One who gives also receives, or can at least expect to receive something in return: status, identity, power, glory. Those who pay for art – whether they are the consumer, patron, sovereign or government – should thereby understand that art is not only on the receiving end of the line, but also the giving. Therein lies the targeted function of art. Mazarin understood this like no other, and Louis XIV showed himself to be an exemplary student.

22.   As the ancients sang

Our relationship with music is partly determined by the ways in which music has been theorised and written about over the centuries. For more than 2,500 years people have studied the possible functions of music: how we relate to music, how we respond to it and what it means to us, but also what its origins are, and its place in a bigger narrative. There are four main views on music which were largely defined in the ancient world and which have determined our thinking about music ever since. To make things easy, I connect these visions with the people who formulated them – Pythagoras, Plato, Aristotle, and Aristoxenos together with Epicure (Epikouros) – but also because hardly any new insights have been developed to the present day.

The oldest and perhaps also the most elemental thinker about music was Pythagoras. He was a mathematician from the sixth century BC who searched for absolute truths in the heavenly firmament that have their effect here on Earth. His name may represent not a single person but a group, a school of thinkers and researchers. Be that as it may, we use the name Pythagoras. He saw a direct connection between music and the proportions in the cosmos. The circular orbits of the planets passing each other would bring forth sounds: the 'harmony of the spheres'. This is purely theoretical music, a musical abstraction. We cannot hear the harmony of the spheres (according to Aristotle, the sound of this would be so loud that everything would be destroyed). Later, in Christian writings, this would be interpreted as the 'musica mundana', the heavenly music that is closest to God. This also explains the prominent position of music theoreticians as ideal musicians until the 17th century. In addition, vocal music and finally instrumental music were given a lower ranking.

The main starting point of Pythagoras's musical theory is the insight that the distances between the Earth, the Sun and the planets can be expressed in numbers which, with their underlying proportions, can in turn be found in the distances between notes, or their intervals, and between the length of a string and its pitch. The relationship between these factors – the proportions in the cosmos and the proportions of the vibrations in a string – almost gives the 'theory' of Pythagoras the character of an absolute or at least a higher truth. Substitute the cosmos for the concept of God or of a divine law, and the Christian Church was provided with an effective argument to connect elements such as the Holy Trinity with music. The result of this was that the three-part time signature was perceived as perfect, and in composing, the only acceptable harmonies were the three elementary intervals of the octave, fifth and fourth.

As far as music was concerned, Pythagoras was particularly interested in mathematical proportions: a combination of the logic of numbers (he was, after all, a mathematician), the certainty of the cosmos and the natural (and physical) origins of the most important intervals and scales. All of this can be traced back to ratios, to numerical and mathematical proportions. This also applies to the supposition that the human brain functions in direct relation to the eternal laws of the cosmos, however abstract that sounds. In the book *Phaedo,* the narrative takes place on the last day of Socrates's life, and in it Plato cites Pythagoras's vision through the words of Simmias of Thebes. Amongst Simmias's statements is the argument that, as opposed to the mortal body, the soul, which remains, is comparable with the harmony that can be heard from a lyre (there is no harmony without a lyre). According to Pythagoras, the 'ratio' of the soul has a direct connection with the 'ratio' of the harmony of the spheres, and in the same sense also with the ratio of the harmonies and tones of the lyre. Hence it is only a small step to the musical-philosophical insights of Plato and Aristotle.

To Plato and Aristotle, music is essentially an echo; a reflection or 'mimesis'. Of course the question is of what, and with which consequences. Plato connects the ratio of music to the ratio of the spirit or the soul. The concept of the ratio of the spirit, even if reality is more complex, could be clarified with the following expression: a bird is known by its note, and a man by his talk. For Plato this means: every bird sings in the way in which its soul and its spirit are put together. On the one hand, the soul has a parallel with the cosmic order, like Pythagoras's harmony of the spheres, and on the other hand, with the specific characteristics of the human whose soul it concerns. Music is not only a reflection of the spirit, but conversely also has its influence on the spirit. Plato can therefore attach an important moral value to music.

However, music existed on broader terms for the Greek philosophers than those we use today. *Mousike* is the entirety of human spiritual expressions, and therefore includes poetry and dance: everything that is offered to us by the gods through the muses. All of these gifts are a reflection of the person to whom they have been given, of his spirit, his nature, his habits, and therefore of his ethos. It is precisely because of this interaction between what we bring forth and what at the same time we can be influenced by that Plato's philosophy has played such an important role through many centuries and into the present day. Thus in the third book of the *Politeia,* the philosopher Socrates and Plato's brother Glaucon discuss the nature of certain keys or modes (ways of organising musical notes). Socrates asks which modes are lamenting in character, or relaxing. Glaucon replies that these are the Lydian and Ionic modes. But which modes are suitable for brave men? These are rather the Doric, and especially the Phrygian.

Clearly, the keys or modes are being connected to the characters of people here. Thus, the Phrygian key was once seen as a reflection of the Phrygian man, known for being fierce and brave. Plato broadens this explanation to include every brave man, from whichever origin, as being connected to the Phrygian mode. Socrates and Plato thus saw mode and character as reciprocal. Therefore, you could also assume that the ratio of the Phrygian scale in essence comes out of the Phrygian spirit. If we take it a step further, then this can imply that an Ionian person needs only to hear or perform music based on the Phrygian scale to undergo a change in his spirit: he becomes a little bit Phrygian.

The direct result of such a vision is, as we can read in the fourth book of the *Politeia,* as recorded by Plato from the mouth of Socrates, that by changing the fundamental keys or modes of a society, the basis of that same society, which after all consists of fundamental laws, is likewise changed.

In *Nomoi* (The Laws), Plato takes a next step in his logical reasoning. He describes the bad influence that music can exert on the spirit when it is practised in a bad way. Here he is not occupied with music in absolute terms, but rather in the craft of the musician. At the same time he points out the influence that bad music can have on the spirit, since the harmony of an individual spirit can then become disturbed. We need to see the harmony of the spirit as the appropriate and correct ratio of that spirit: the bird that is known by its note. When it sings differently it becomes a different bird. Plato realised that it was not realistic to reject entirely what in his eyes were 'bad' modes, or modes which are derived from bad spirits, bad characters and bad habits. There will always be other people in addition to Dorians and Phrygians.

Nevertheless, as a true moralist and with his finger raised, Plato warns time and again against the influence of bad music, not only on the individual but also on the entire State and the public authorities. He even goes as far as to want to ban by law the use of erroneous music at important occasions such as religious ceremonies or public events. As far as Plato is concerned, those who perform the wrong hymns before the gods can be excluded from such ceremonies and prosecuted for their wickedness. In Plato's vision, hymns were to be constructed according to clear principles, which should incidentally also apply to dances. Therefore he put heavy moral pressure on both the makers and the users of music. It is this moralistic side to his thinking about music which we later find in Christianity, but equally in politically totalitarian systems such as the Soviet Union, the German Democratic Republic and China under Maoism. Everything is determined from the top down: what kind of music is good and bad for people, divine and diabolical, positive and negative; which music is permitted, and that which is not.

Aristotle is less the schoolmaster and more the inquisitive researcher. He is fundamentally different from Plato in that he does not believe something like music can change the ratio of the spirit in a person. Aristotle distinguishes between virtues and skills. What the muses have given us are skills such as music. Aristotle sees 'virtue', however, as a static capacity and *mousike* as a combination of skills that can and must be developed through good education. A good training in music, poetry, dance and sport is of great importance for the forming of every child into a man. Thus, in Aristotle's vision music is dynamic, and in that of Plato it is more static. At the same time Aristotle sees skills as less elevated than virtues. Even worse, virtuosity is in a certain way vulgar, or plebeian. But he has to admit that music can give pleasure, even if this does not mean that it can influence us.

Aristotle could not deny that daily practice was less simple than the theory: in particular, the instrumental music used in the tragedies had become highly virtuoso and was remarkably popular, too. He regarded this with the analytical mind of a sociologist. Searching for the functionality of music, he divided the keys or modes into three categories, namely moral, practical and emotional. The first category is suitable in upbringing and can improve a person; the second initiates action, bringing spirit and body into motion; and the third ensures excitement and relaxation. In this way, Aristotle focused more on the social use of music than on giving it moralistic functions. He established that music is a reflection, an imitation or mimesis of what is happening in society. At the same time he paved the way to further study of the relationship between music and emotion, and in particular the different emotional responses that music can inspire in people.

No less important is the distinction that Aristotle makes between higher and lower art: art with a high moral level, which is good for education, and art for relaxation. This concept became more prominent in the course of the 19th century, when a clearer dichotomy gradually arose between concert music and music for entertainment. In Germany, an oft-used distinction is between *E-Musik* and *U-Musik*; 'Ernste Musik' and 'Unterhaltungsmusik'. The first of these should have artistic value (think of Aristotle's first category), and the second is intended only for general enjoyment (Aristotle's third category). When we apply this dichotomy in a social sense, too, we could assume that the upper classes (who have had a fine moral education, to use Aristotle's terms) produce and consume *E-Musik*, the lower classes *U-Musik*. Thus, music had become a reflection of the social classes.

The next two philosophers, Aristoxenos and Epicure, have in common that they wanted to assess music only with the ear and not as a part of any cosmic, political or sociological truth. Aristoxenos regarded music as an entirely isolated phenomenon. Music is not the same as mathematics, since you cannot hear mathematical proportions and numbers. However, you can hear and absorb musical notes with your senses, the ears, and relate them to each other with or without help from the memory. Aristoxenos took an entirely empirical viewpoint, just through listening. He also pointed out that the reality of music bears no relation to any other reality. Music is wholly itself, and is the reflection only of itself. With this notion, Aristoxenos was a distant forerunner of the phenomenological and formalistic perception of music.

In the second century AD, Claudius Ptolemaeus merged the theories of Pythagoras and Plato with those of Aristoxenos, since to his mind empiric research had proved that both the ear and the mind, both the senses and knowledge of mathematical proportions, are needed to be able to assess music. However, when we do establish that music can only be of itself and exists only through the grace of our senses, what is then the purpose of music? The Roman poet Lucretius, who preserved a large part of the thinking of Epicure for us in the 1st Century BC, took a closer look at this in the fourth book of *De rerum natura* (On the nature of things). What do these sounds mean to us? According to Epicure, music can do little more than trigger sensual pleasure. He distinguished two kinds of pleasure: active and static. The first kind concerns the pleasure that occurs while listening to a beautiful piece of music, the second is the pleasure that comes afterwards, when you are fulfilled by having listened, and which therefore arises through the memory of the music which you have heard. He considered the latter a higher form of enjoyment than the first. With the first only the senses, the ears, are touched, and the pleasure remains exclusively there. With the second, the pleasure can occur throughout the entire body.

Although Epicure had a materialistic view on music – that it consists merely of sounds – the idea of a higher form of pleasure is a phenomenon we come across once again in discussions of transcendent experiences when listening. For many music lovers, the purest musical enjoyment is the result of listening to the sublime sounds of an abstract composition. Sound for sound's sake. Beautiful melodies just for the sake of beautiful melodies. In other words, a piece of music as an object in its own right. Sceptics such as Pyrrho and Sextus Empiricus even went a step further than Epicure, by concluding that all music is purely a figment of the mind. It is impossible for music to be the subject of any kind of intellectual engagement since it has no tangible form or concrete reality, but only what we perceive through our ears. This is the so-called ontological approach, the essence of which would later be found in the writings of Immanuel Kant.

Outlined above are four substantial ways of thinking about music: the mathematical line from Pythagoras, the ethical and pedagogical from Socrates and Plato, the sociological from Aristotle and the empirical phenomenological of Aristoxenos and Epicure. For the first three, the relationship between music and the laws of the cosmos is inseparably present, even if the interpretations differ with regard to its influence. Thereafter this relationship is increasingly brought into doubt, however, even if one can never quite avoid the connection between scales and harmonies on the one hand and certain 'natural' laws at the other. Around the first century AD, music in Greco-Roman society gradually became the subject of mere pleasure. This was a thorn in the side of early Christian theologians, for whom pleasure played no role in the quest for redemption. They therefore had to find a way of bending the theories of the ancient world to their own theological insights. The ideas of Pythagoras, Plato and Aristotle lent themselves better to this than those of the later philosophers, and in this way the first great thinkers from the ancient world laid a strong foundation for more than two thousand years of Western musical philosophy and culture.

The theories of Pythagoras have lost little of their strength and directness into our own times. Music continued to be a part of the quadrivium until well into the 18th century, together with arithmetic, geometry and astronomy. During part of the 19th and the early 20th centuries, this position seemed to have been overshadowed by a strong craving for a music that is purely emotionally and intuitively composed. Most composers recognised this as a fictional image created by outsiders, and not that of their own reality at the writing desk. Composing is a combination of architecture, mathematics, linguistics and psychology, but then in sound. Over the last hundred years Pythagorean thinking about music has become extremely important in music, and not only with the arrival of computers and numerous new, more cerebral compositional techniques. In general we have become more aware that the composing of music (and equally its performance) requires considerable mathematical ability: to solidify the logic of music into real sound, to give structure to time, to make music rise above the phenomenon of mere sound.

Plato's philosophical insights have also remained almost entirely unchanged in our times. His collection of ideas, but even more the way in which he explains the influence of music on the mind, resulted in the first few centuries AD in the fledgling Church of Rome putting much emphasis on the need to avoid any tendency for physicality in music (the fewer emotions the better), and to set the 'idea' of music higher than the actual music itself.

Therefore, the abstract 'musica mundana', the theory of music and the harmony of the (heavenly or divine) spheres, was central to this contemplation and appreciation of music. However, no one could ignore the fact that there was singing in church. The 'idea' of sound had its physical reality, a reflection in the real world. This is the 'musica instrumentalis', the sounding music. In order to keep singing in church as understated as possible there nevertheless began a lengthy period of mainly theoretical wrangling. All music had to be focused on the confessional. Outside the Church, the situation was of course entirely different, even though there, too, one realised that the rules for composing music were principally intended to pursue a higher good: the higher in artistry and the higher in art. To say nothing, lastly, about music intended for dancing.

Step by step, in the course of the 14th and 15th centuries the path was laid from music as an imitation of divine nature – the Platonic idea of music as abstraction – to music as a concrete expression of words and emotions. Nevertheless, the Platonic school of thought continued to play a significant role in this. Indeed, Plato warned about the negative influence of less elevated music on the human spirit, as did the Church from its own dogmas, but society, especially the nobility and wealthy citizens, wanted to be able to express in music the many facets of human emotion, even if these were not always particularly lofty in nature. But this did not drive Plato from the stage. Up until well into the 20th century, people accepted the situation as it presented itself: there was higher and lower music, music for the Church and for the street, for the nobility and for the state. And indeed, such a sociological division certainly contained a judgement about quality, too.

During the second half of the 18th century the ethical (but no less Platonic) view on the need for mainly lofty or sublime music was superseded by an increasingly aesthetic attitude. The main result, however, was that with the concept of taste as central focus, people could only really argue with each other through criticism of each other's taste. And then in the 20th century, Plato was suddenly back in the picture when, as has already been said, totalitarian systems (the Third Reich, the Soviet Union, the GDR and the People's Republic of China) determined which music could and could not be composed and performed. This was all under the pretext of protecting the metal health of the populace against bad influences. From the Christian viewpoint Plato also reappeared, for example when certain kinds of pop music were condemned as being the work of the Devil.

23. The history of the history of music

> And untill a set of musicall vertuosi, well weighed in a resolution, and capable to make the experiment, and of whom none, as thinking themselves wiser, shall put on the contemptuous frowne and seem inwardly to sneer, shall be mett together, with all things fitt for the same designe, there will be no reason to expect the antiquitys of musick should ever be understood.

So wrote the English nobleman and amateur musician Roger North at the beginning of the 18th century. He was looking for ways to understand the music of the past, but his conclusion was that something would first have to change with musicians themselves.

Something was indeed happening in London at that time: perhaps not exactly what North had in mind, but a first step nevertheless. In the *Crown and Anchor* on the Strand there were regular meetings of a group of music lovers who were dedicated to the study and performance of vocal music from the 16th and 17th centuries under the name of the Academy of Vocal Music, and later the Academy of Ancient Music. They were of course particularly interested in the music of the glorious Elizabethan period, but also in works from a time that wasn't so very far removed from their own, namely that of the composer of the collection of songs *Orpheus Britannicus*, Henry Purcell.

One of the founders of this circle of amateurs was Dr. John Christopher Pepusch, also known as the composer from Berlin, Johann Christoph Pepusch. Works on the programme included those by Thomas Tallis, William Byrd, Giovanni da Palestrina and indeed Henry Purcell. Also included was the Italian Archangelo Corelli, who had died at the beginning of the century and whose *Concerti grossi* were very popular in England, and remained so for the entire 18th century. In Pepusch's homeland, people had never entirely lost sight of the music of the late Renaissance, such as the works of Palestrina. These remained the subject of study until well into the 18th century for anyone who pursued a thorough knowledge of music theory. This explains why Palestrina's polyphony was a part of the important textbook *Gradus ad Parnassum* of 1725, by Johann Joseph Fux.

This natural link with the past was broken, however, during the second half of the century. Johann Sebastian Bach still used the music theory of the late Renaissance and the early 17th century as a resource, but even during his lifetime people considered this remarkably old-fashioned. A mere generation later and the break with the past was complete. The elegant music that became popular with the nobility and citizens around 1750 had nothing – musically, technically or ethically – to do with the scholarly techniques of the 16th and 17th centuries. During Bach's lifetime, people had great difficulties with his predilection for his musical ancestors, and by 1780 the study of his music had become a mostly historical occupation. It seemed that people were already aware that with 'old' Bach, an era was over.

The past and the history of bygone times still had its allure, however. In 1752 with his *Allgemeine Geschichtswissenschaft*, Johann Martin Chladenius sounded the starting pistol for scientific research of history as a subject. Not long after this Johann Joachim Winckelmann wrote the first essays about the archaeology of the ancient world. In the 1780s, Johann Wolfgang von Goethe travelled to Italy and visited Pompeii to see the remains of antique culture with his own eyes. Not only the sunny country ('where the lemon trees bloom') on the other side of the Alps attracted so many, but also the culture of days long gone, represented by those radiant white chunks of temples and the remains of cities emerging from the ground, especially in Southern Italy.

What people encountered in Italy and Greece in those days led to a view of the ancient world as a culture of timeless white beauty. We now have to concede that this is a romantic image, divorced from reality. After all, Greek and Roman temples were originally brightly painted. In the later 19th century, this romanticised picture of the ancient world combined with the perception of Mozart as a classicist composer *par excellence*, and this in part led to the presentation of the genius who died at such a young age as a 'white angel': his music considered as radiant as those Hellenistic temples, his person pictured as a little rococo angel in his snow-white costume and wig. This was Mozart as the personification of an ideal of classical music: as idyllic and Arcadian as the dreamed worlds of Watteau. Thus, by 1900, Mozart had almost become a fairy-tale character when compared with the tumultuous violence of the music of the time. Hadn't Kant claimed that music belonged to a world that was different from that of physical things?

In the middle of the 18th century the first editions of the *Historisch-kritischen Beyträge zur Aufname der Musik* appeared, a magazine edited by Friedrich Wilhelm Marpurg. This reported comprehensively on musical life in France, the Germanic countries and Italy, as well as looking back to developments in what was then known as early music, such as old instruments, music theory of the past and interesting discoveries in the field of music. There was no really coherent historical narrative yet, but curiosity about the past had clearly become an important driving force. Unfortunately, after five years the magazine ceased to exist.

In the same period, the Italian music theoretician Giovanni Battista Martini, also known as Padre Martini, had conceived a plan to write a history of music from the earliest times to his own present day. Of this *Storia della Musica* (1757, 1770 and 1781) he only completed three parts. In these he covered the history of music since the days of Adam and Eve, right through the Old Testament, the fundamentals of music theory including that of the ancient world, monophonic liturgical chants, counterpoint, the various kinds of voices and so on. All of this was richly founded on the sources known at the time. A fourth part about music in the 11th century exists only partially as a sketch.

Padre Martini also collected a volume of old Italian and Spanish polyphonic works (especially by Palestrina and Da Victoria) under the revealing title *Esemplare di contrappunto* (1775), or examples of counterpoint, with the addition of associated rules as taken by Martini in part from Fux. A few years before the publication of this volume, the young Mozart came to Bologna with his father in order to learn counterpoint with Padre Martini. He did an aptitude test and was given a pass, 'given the circumstances'. Actually, Mozart's exercises were not that good, but Martini understood that the young genius was capable of doing other things better than anyone else. In any case, Mozart's counterpoint would turn out to be perfectly fine after he had studied the works of the great Bach in the 1780s.

Even more important was the publication by French composer and philosopher Jean-Jacques Rousseau of a *Dictionnaire de Musique* in 1767. Unlike the majority of his German and Italian colleagues, Rousseau elected to keep his *Dictionnaire* strictly alphabetical rather than giving a systematic ranking order. He therefore starts with 'A mi la, A la mi re, ou simplement A,' which he defines as: 'The sixth tone of the diatonic and natural scale, which is otherwise also called "la".' He finishes after more than seven hundred pages with 'ZA. Syllabe par laquelle on distingue, dans le Plain-Chant, le Si Bémol du Si naturel auquel on laisse le nom de Si.' To clarify this description: in plainchant the distinction between Si bémol, by which is meant the *B-flat*, and Si naturel, the *B*, is denoted by calling the first Za and the second Si. All of the terms, theoretical concepts and musical genres known at the time are covered in a clear and concise way. Rousseau had collated the very first music encyclopaedia.

Music history had by now become a respectable subject, even if the way in which the past was classified and described was more theoretical, technical and mathematical (both in terms of cosmology and tonal genera as well as acoustics) than stylistic. There were no broad outlines, and broad connections were not made.

Hence in 1770, the young composer Nicolas-Étienne Framery published a schematic overview of the then state of knowledge and insight in a *Tableau de la musique et de ses branches*, in which all of the musical disciplines are accommodated and arranged hierarchically by importance. Acoustics were at the top for Framery (in this, Mersenne, Saveur and others had preceded him), as well as practical music (we would call this the theory of composing and performing) and history (a merging of the description of the music of yesteryear in a general sense, and of music as something produced by people).

The German theologian Martin Gerbert published three adventurous volumes in 1784, the *Scriptores ecclesiastici de musica sacra,* with an overview of composers and especially music theoreticians from the third century onwards. In England, too, various books were dedicated to the history of music. After sixteen years of hard work, John Hawkins released the first volume of a five-part *General History of the Science and Practice of Music* in 1776. That same year, Charles Burney also made himself heard with the first part of his three-volume *General History of Music*. In France the bulky *Essai sur la musique ancienne et moderne* (1780) appeared in four volumes by Jean-Benjamin De Laborde, of course with much attention given to French music, and in Germany there was the *Allgemeine Geschichte der Musik* (1788-1801) by Johann Nikolaus Forkel.

While, as is indicated by the title, De Laborde dealt with music until his own time, Forkel never reached the finishing line in that regard. In part due to his exhaustive approach, he never made it further in his listings than Heinrich Isaac at the beginning of the 16th century. Forkel's description of a three-part canon by Johannes Ockeghem is a good example of the way in which early historians had to work with the materials they had to hand. His copy of the canon looks rather abstract, without words and with all those long note values. What Forkel didn't know was that the canon in fact is based on a chanson: *Prenez sur moi vostre exemple amoureux*. This chanson was originally notated on a single stave, but given symbols from which can be elucidated that it is a canon

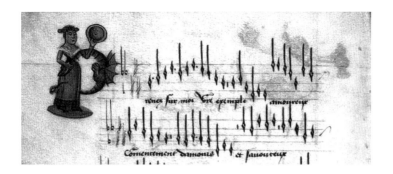

21. Johannes Ockeghem, *Prenez sur moi vostre exemple amoureux*, ms Thott 291 8⁰, 39 verso, Det Kongelige Bibliotek, Copenhagen. Take note of the flats and sharps at the front of the stave: first two flats, one under the other, then a flat and under that a sharp and finally two sharps. Each pair gives the pitch and therefore the modality with which the same notation leads to a three-part canon.

22. Idem, as printed in Johann Nikolaus Forkel's *Allgemeine Geschichte der Musik*, part 2. Ockeghem is called Ockenheim here, but is also known as Jean d'Ockenheim or Okegus.

for performance by three singers, each with their own key. That sounds not only rather complicated, but it took musical science a long time and plenty of headaches to arrive at a satisfactory solution to Ockeghem's musical puzzle.

Forkel, who incidentally was using an incorrect version of the notation (borrowed from Charles Burney), didn't consider the composition to be particularly beautiful: 'It is and remains stiff and not singable'. Although he considered Ockeghem to be the Bach of his time, the impenetrability of Ockeghem's notation (in part the consequence of a wrong solution to the puzzle), and therefore for Forkel also the impenetrability of the music itself, stood in the way of an enjoyment of art which strives for beauty

23. Idem, in the version by Charles Burney as printed in Forkel's *Allgemeine Geschichte der Musik*. While with Ockeghem this is clearly a chanson with a French text, Burney and Forkel assumed that the composition was a three-part (trium vocum) fugue. The voices enter three notes after each other, and each time a fifth lower.

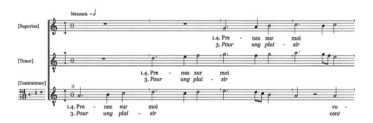

24. Idem, in a version by Peter Woetmann Christoffersen, 2009. In this case the voices enter a fourth higher each time. The result can immediately be heard in the harmonies.

and good taste. With regard to this, the music of the Bach of his own time was far superior.

The notation of Bach's music was indeed less enigmatic, and the facts of his life were also considerably less shrouded in mystery than Ockeghem's in the 15th century. Forkel therefore gave Bach all his attention. His first substantial biography appeared in 1802: *Über J.S. Bachs Leben, Kunst und Kunstwerke*. In this he worked as a genuine researcher, gaining first-hand information by speaking to Bach's sons, Carl Philipp Emanuel and Wilhelm Friedemann, investigating the works of the master which were known to him (and that was a considerable quantity), and consulting numerous sources from Bach's own time, studying the music of his predecessors, contemporaries and pupils. This was not only due to the artful pleasure provided by Bach's music, but above all because in his opinion it was of national importance that he should take on this Titanic task.

Most 18th-century authors and researchers were more interested in collecting music-theoretical data than providing an overview of composers and their individual characteristics within a historical context. With his major study on Bach's life and music, Forkel had therefore produced pioneering work. With the knowledge and standards of his time, he attempted a judgement based on aesthetic qualities.

By 1800 music was clearly in a transitional area between the already centuries-old 'scientia' or theoretical science on the one hand, and the phenomenon of taste or 'Geschmack', as it was known to Forkel and his German-speaking colleagues, on the other. Good taste was connected to an understanding of beauty, which in the end led to a distinction between diverse musical styles, each with their own expressions of beauty. Forkel was not yet concerned with a quest to understand the personalities of the composers, and to what extent these determined the beauty of their works as individuals, but rather with the theoretical foundations upon which each composer cemented the next stone, and some even numerous stones on top of each other. He therefore remained quite close to the 'scientia'.

In 1792 Forkel published an *Allgemeine Litteratur der Musik, oder Anleitung zur Kenntniss musikalischer Bücher, welche von den ältesten bis auf die neusten Zeiten bey den Griechen, Römern und den meisten neuern europäischen Nationen sind geschrieben worden.* This is a mouthful of a title, which indicates that this is an extensive and exhaustive encyclopaedic summary of everything written on music history as it was then known, from the ancient Greeks to the 1770s. Similar handbooks already existed, but on a much smaller scale. Even the table of contents of Forkel's overview is impressive. In each chapter there are lists of summaries about what had been written on and theorised about music since creation. Forkel proceeded thoroughly in this, from generalities to details, from overviews of overviews written by others, to overviews of music by numerous peoples.

Just as with Marpurg, Gerbert and Hawkins, the music of the Hebrews from the Old Testament, and of the Egyptians, Greeks and Romans, is meticulously summed up based on sources and earlier writings on those sources. Very slowly something akin to a storyline also creeps in, although Forkel principally remains in typical 18th-century methodological mode, scattering an encyclopaedic quantity of titles of sources, writings and sometimes dates over the reader. We can now see that the amount of material available at the time must have been immense. Forkel and his predecessors, on whom he often builds with his overview of literature, must have travelled widely through town and country, from monastery to city archive, from castle library to chapter-school to assemble such extensive lists. In addition, where possible, Forkel provides a short description of every source, as was common practice then in the 'catalogues raisonnés'.

Forkel also mentions a number of Dutch handbooks, such as that by Wilhelm Lustig, who provided Leopold Mozart with the translation for his violin method. In the field of instrumental textbooks we also find here, alongside Leopold Mozart's original publication, several books for learning how to play the harmonica, or the musette (a small set of bagpipes). In the fifth chapter of the second part of his *Allgemeine Litteratur der Musik* Forkel covers an extensive list of sources and tracts about composing itself. This is an overview of everything that had been written *about* composing. Artusi, Mersenne, Werckmeister, Fux, Scheibe, Geminiani, Marpurg, Kirnberger and Rousseau; we encounter them all here, and with this, Forkel laid the foundation for the later discipline of musicology.

After 1800, research into the history of music increasingly gained momentum, and three decades later, so did research into the lives of the composers. The new middle class had a great need to construct its own cultural identity and its own history. Historical novels were supposed to make the past a reality, a past in which the citizens had taken no less an active part than the nobility. But while the nobility only had to look around them, to their estates, their castles, the walls of which were covered with paintings of many generations of ancestors, the rapidly developing bourgeoisie had to convert the rights and ideals acquired since the French Revolution and Napoleon into historical facts. For that reason alone there was an urgent need for research into the past, an ever more substantial past, in search of an increasingly shared culture.

Not only music theoreticians, but also philologists and historians went in search of the sources and products of their own culture. They were committed to bringing the old music back to life, and unlike their predecessors in the 18th century they strove to present the results of this research in concert practice. The music had to sound once again. Even in the 1780s, Johann Adam Hiller and Mozart had made new concert versions of Handel's *Messiah*. (Mozart's version provoked one critic to remark that it was comparable with 'stucco ornaments on a marble temple', or in other words, like putting rococo angels onto the Parthenon.) What Hiller and Mozart were pursuing was no different from what Mendelssohn wanted to achieve in 1829 with Bach's *Matthäus Passion*: that the audiences of their day could accept and learn to appreciate such masterpieces.

When Mendelssohn and Schumann arranged Bach's work (and, for instance, added a piano part to the sonatas for solo violin or the cello suites), they did this out of anything but a sense of dissatisfaction with the original appearance of the music, as if they were of the opinion that Bach could be improved: on the contrary. They were merely looking for ways of making Bach's music more accessible. In this they had a different vision to that of Ferruccio Busoni in about 1900. He was of the opinion that Bach had not been able to achieve what he had wanted, since not all of the technical means had been at his disposal. Busoni therefore filled in Bach's harmonic language here and there with the developments of his own time. He sincerely hoped that in this way, justice would be done and full expression brought to the hidden intentions of composers from the past, doing both them and their audiences a service.

Busoni's method is to a certain extent comparable with that of conductors such as Mahler or Mengelberg, when they retouched the instrumentation and sometimes even the harmonies in the scores of others. How often was it thought – and frequently still is – that Schumann was unable to orchestrate, at least not at Beethoven's level, and that it was therefore necessary to 'correct' Schumann's scores? The aim was in the service of composers, even though nowadays we consider these changes to be unauthorised and inauthentic. As far as Busoni is concerned, we have to realise that as a pianist and educator he made a tremendous contribution to the performance of Bach's keyboard works in the modern editions and arrangements he released.

The new performing scores that were produced in the late 18th and a large part of the 19th centuries were mainly intended to make music resoundingly accessible for people of the time. In fact, the conductor Leopold Stokowski was doing exactly the same thing when he arranged Bach's music for a large orchestra in the 1920s and 1930s. In order to evaluate these 'arrangements', whether they were made in the 1840s or the 1920s, it is necessary to take the listener's musical taste into consideration, as well as the most appropriate ways to open their ears to older music. In around 1840 a solo violin was considered 'bare', and much of Bach's music too learned and complex. The works of Giovanni Gabrieli and Palestrina sounded 'strange' to many people due to their lack of 'real' melodies and their floating harmonies. Not everything could be arranged straightforwardly. Bach and his contemporaries were better suited to this than the composers of the 16th century. Thus, it was more effective to concentrate on studying mainly the techniques of the latter, and to use these for a 'new' music.

In the first half of the 19th century numerous studies were written about Palestrina, Lassus, Gabrieli and their contemporaries;

and in the second half of the century many musical works were composed in particular for the Roman Catholic liturgy, in which attempts were made to revive the world of these 16th-century masters. However, this was not only done for the often so incomprehensible 'old' music. What was valid for Monteverdi, Bach or Handel was also valid for the symphonies of Beethoven, the songs of Schubert or the operas of Carl Maria von Weber, to name just a few. The possibilities for performing these works were scarce. There were too few good orchestras and not enough good singers or opera companies. So these works too had to be adapted, reworked, arranged or re-orchestrated.

A piano virtuoso such as Liszt would therefore tour all over Europe performing songs by Schubert, the symphonies of Beethoven and operas by Mozart, not only in virtuoso transcriptions for piano, but also in the form of variations on themes from these works or as fantasies, a kind of musical contemplations. Music lovers increasingly bought the symphonies of Mozart, Haydn, Beethoven and later Schubert, Brahms, Bruckner and Mahler, too, in all kinds of arrangements for piano solo, piano duet or piano trio. Much music did the rounds in this way, some pieces being more faithful to the original than others, but ultimately all of them variants which significantly differed from what the composer must originally have intended, and which were certainly further removed from the original than a well-painted copy of a Titian or Rembrandt.

During the 19th century, researchers became aware that the past had produced works of art of great value. Because of this, the judgement of contemporary art was increasingly measured against the greatness of those works from earlier times. Historical research into the old masters was considered of great interest, especially for a better positioning of contemporary expressions of art. Palestrina, Schütz, Bach and Handel, and after 1850 also Haydn, Mozart and Beethoven, stood as a reference against which the quality of new music could be measured. As a result, music history became increasingly a comparative science, with style and technique but also sublimity or power of expression as important yardsticks. Taste and knowledge competed for supremacy, with art historians, philologists and music theoreticians leading the way.

Thus the great story arose in the course of that century, the continuous line, the obvious path of development from the one great master to the next. Palestrina and Bach as founding fathers of our Western music, with Bach also standing as the apotheosis of 'old' music. He closed one developmental line and laid the first stone for new one, in which Haydn, Mozart and Beethoven swiftly reached great heights. And since a significant part of music-historical research was done in Germany, the cultural history that was put on record there was mainly focused on its own musical developments: it supported the conviction that German culture surpassed all others. This research was therefore indeed a matter of national importance, just as Forkel had concluded with regard to his Bach explorations.

Although the science of music history in the German-speaking world indeed took flight and certainly held a leading position until the 1950s, other countries did not lag behind. A profusion of mostly nationally-coloured historical surveys arose within a half century, until the beginning of the First World War, precisely because of the desire to inspire and capture national identities also historically and culturally. The field of research became gradually more extensive, too. Country after country was brought onto the map, and century after century was sifted. More and more branches had to be added to the main historical lines as a result of the multitude of information, and the history of art (music, literature and the visual arts) of the 20th century became ever more finely categorised. One thing, however, remained almost unchanged from the beginning of the last century to the present: that single line. It all began with the rise of Christianity, and from there every phase is a logical continuation of the previous one.

Thus the history of music was presented as a continuous narrative from Classical antiquity to modern music after 1900. After all, styles and techniques changed over the centuries, and since art historians had by then already determined that the period following ancient culture should be known as the 'dark' middle ages, and that this period had made place for the Renaissance by 1400, and that the Renaissance was followed by the Baroque in about 1600, and that in the middle of the 18th century the Baroque was overtaken by a rapid accumulation of new expressions under names such as Rococo and Sturm und Drang, and subsequently by Rationalism, which in its turn made way for Romanticism, music historians meekly followed the same route. In fact, it was only in the 1970s that the question was posed as to whether this vision was correct, or if we imagined our conclusions too crudely or one-sidedly. Since then, the history of music has regularly been 'adjusted'.

Many of these adjustments have to do with changing views on the material itself: the music, the sources, the theoretical writings, but also with the exponential growth of research areas, with new research techniques and with new insights into the phenomenon of history in its own right. With regard to music, these changing views are also connected to a new look at the function of music in society, to the way people have made use of music through the centuries. Thus music history was first determined by a chain of theoretical discourses (until into the 19th century), and subsequently by a succession of musical styles and their composers. In the first half of the 20th century the research area was expanded into the functionality of music, into music sociology. Within this discipline one sees composers as children of their time, as products of the society from which they evolve and in which they live and work. Composers no longer float as strange creatures above the world of ordinary people, but have become an integrated part of it.

At the same time, people became aware that the correct way of describing the past, and the music of the past, is not served by looking backwards. If we want to understand Bach or Mozart, and want to fathom what they might have meant to their own times, then we need to approach Bach's music from Sweelinck,

Schein or Pachelbel, and Mozart's from Gluck, Haydn and Johann Christian Bach. My teacher, Professor Eduard Reeser, once asked us students to listen for an entire year exclusively to music composed before 1760, and only then to take on a work by Mozart. We would literally fall off our chairs! Playing Bach with Brahms in mind says virtually nothing about Bach and a great deal about Brahms. This is what brought Frans Brüggen to state, at the end of the 1960s, that every note of Mozart played by the Concertgebouw Orchestra was a lie. At that time, the members of the orchestra still had to learn what it meant to perform Mozart with Mozart's sound-world in their ears.

Even the hegemony of Western culture as such was called into question in the last century. Intensive research by ethnomusicologists into the music of 'foreign' peoples provided scientific insight into other cultures (which were therefore no longer considered as strange and exotic, as they would have been long before), and also changed views on the development of much early Western European music. In the same way that Bartók and Kodály strove to retain the original values of the folk music of the Hungarian and Romanian countryside, and thus not to edit it but to capture it as faithfully as possible for posterity, the musical traditions and techniques from Indonesia, Japan, India and numerous African and South-American countries, for example, were put on the map by ethnomusicologists and anthropologists. We can trace the influence of these in contemporary Western music throughout the 20th century.

The consequences of this were soon to be seen in the performance practice of very early music. Let me give a single example of this. At the beginning of the 1970s the Studio der frühen Musik was in the Netherlands to give some concerts, and at the end of their tour I brought the four musicians to Schiphol Airport. When their flight turned out to be considerably delayed, the lutenist and musicologist of the ensemble, Thomas Binkley, spontaneously offered to take me for a drink and to explain in detail about the music they had been performing: that of troubadours such as Raimbaut de Vaqueiras and Bernart de Ventadorn. These beautiful songs survive as monophonic melodies and are only partially provided with some text. In musicological lectures at university we were given these in their 'source version', as they were handed down to us, and recordings were played of performances by a single unaccompanied singer. Then came the Studio der frühen Musik as well as recorder player René Clemencic with his ensemble, both with completely different visions on this music. They considered the 12th-century songs as basic material for numerous improvised variants with the original melodies, sometimes sung, sometimes performed by a variety of bowed and plucked string instruments, winds and percussion. This was a colourful affair: a shock for many a musicologist and a festive experience for audiences.

Based on intensive studies, Binkley was of the opinion that the troubadours must have been strongly influenced by the Arabic culture that prevailed in a considerable part of the Iberian Peninsula and the southern Provencal regions of France until into the 15th century. He therefore chose a sound that is closely linked to the Arabic music that can still be heard in North Africa today. Clemencic looked for something closer to home. In his performances of the surviving songs from that time, he showed that it would have been impossible for itinerant musicians to have performed their sung narratives unaccompanied and as bare as church chants. In images from the period we see all kinds of people festooned with drums, wind and string instruments. Whether they were at court or at some fair, it would often have been a colourful spectacle. In short, where studies initially concentrated on the monophonic musical sources, people ultimately had to recognise that what was written down could be no more than a guide or a reminder. The music which actually sounded was largely improvised, a tradition which was part of even the most serious music until far into the 18th century.

On the basis of these kinds of experiences, as well as on the basis of research into the music of other cultures and, as far as Europe is concerned, especially those cultures that were within easy reach (those of North Africa and the Middle East), one can understand that renewed reflection was needed on the sources of what we so grandly call our Western music. People often behaved as if we had invented the musical wheel. The composer Ton de Leeuw, who has also done intensive study into the music of the Indonesian archipelago, Japan, India and the Arabic world, called the search that he and many others undertook in the 1960s and 1970s 'the way back to the source'. Until deep into the 20th century people always thought that Western music was mainly of Christian origin. Now we are no longer so sure. It is at least fairly realistic to assume that other influences have been at least as important, such as outlined above with regard to the Arabic influence on the troubadours; and that is just one example.

What concerns me the most here is that the certainties that we had fifty years ago no longer exist. Doubt is a good basis for science. In music, too, and with the description of musical developments, doubt has indeed resulted in renewed discussions about the unique development of two thousand years of music in Europe (but also beyond), and many other things. By way of conclusion, let me mention a few points. Were the middle ages really so dark? Or can we now postulate that, also in music, this assumption is largely based on our knowledge of the written sources available? The numerous dialects that emerged from the start within the body of monophonic church hymns, but also for instance the remarkable work of the 12th-century mystic and composer Hildegard von Bingen, are indicative of a musical richness of which many fruits still remain hidden or have been lost.

Did the Renaissance really begin in the early 15th century? Or should we recognise that there was more than just one single Renaissance, also in music? Could it be that what we in the 19th century considered defining characteristics of the Renaissance, namely a greater focus on the human being and the world of ideas, already presented themselves in the 12th century, but that the Church in Rome suppressed such developments with every power at its disposal? And might it be that the musical ideal of the Renaissance was partly fulfilled at the end of the 16th and beginning of the 17th centuries, precisely through the use at that time of those techniques that we now like to see as 'Baroque'? Is it conceivable that history, and therefore music history and perhaps even the whole of cultural history shouldn't be classified on stylistic, but rather on social grounds, and therefore on the use of art and culture in social interaction?

Can we simply imagine that there are in fact such things as music for the Church, music for the aristocracy, music for the citizenry, music for streets and squares, and so on? Maybe we should see the development of music in an entirely different light, anyway: much more anthropological, sociological and philosophical. Then perhaps we will better understand why certain stylistic developments have taken place: because these were needed, because society changed, because there were changes in the use of music. Perhaps in reality only two ways of interacting with music exist, an ethical and an aesthetic: the first as a duty, a necessity, the second because it is fun, pleasant and diverting. Thus we can better understand the differences between Beethoven's piano concertos and symphonies, and the late quartets and piano sonatas; or between Bach's pragmatic attitude as compared to the idealistic strivings of Beethoven or Mahler; or between the Church music and madrigals of Monteverdi. It might also then become clear why one composer was ignored in his own time (as we now believe, unjustly) and the other eulogised (as we now believe, equally unjustly). This has not only to do with style, but more especially with usefulness.

It may be clear that there are no truths in respect of music history; at the most, facts such as dates and sources. Everything else is opinion: mine, yours, that of the scholar or of the reviewer. Not one of these opinions is truer than the other. History, and also music history, is written by people on the basis of facts on the one hand, and opinions and insights on the other. As we have seen, those opinions and insights are anything but constant – any more than is music itself: through the centuries, in innumerable performances, for countless listeners, each with their own insights, views, and ways of using it.

24. By way of an epilogue: music now

In recent decades it has been suggested in newspapers and at symposia that 'classical' music is finished, at least as we know it today. Concert halls are emptying, the symphony orchestra is outdated and traditional concerts are no longer adequate. At the same time, research increasingly shows that humans are musical by nature, and that a life without music is unimaginable. Governments in numerous countries follow the more negative messages and, more than the citizens themselves, put our cultural treasures at risk by withdrawing from their duty of care, a duty which has been taken over from the nobility and the Church in exchange for often substantial taxes. This happens at a time in which more people than ever are engaged with the many facets of art. Is this contradiction – retreating governments and an increasing number of participants – an example of the law of diminishing returns (damage through excess), or do politicians no longer realise the importance of art and culture for a healthy society?

Today's art sector can be compared to a giant supermarket with thousands of products to suit everyone's taste. As far as music is concerned we find everything from religious chant from the 10th century and masterpieces from the music theatre of yesteryear, music from the Midwest, the Far East and Down Under, music for the church, the pub, the street and the living room, folk and ethnic music, choral works and symphonies, pop and film music, muzak, new wave, funk, punk, reggae and rap, extremely complex and very simple music, tonal and atonal music, music based on all kinds of local or national scales and tonal systems, improvised music and computer music, adjacent and all mixed up together. I have no doubt missed out so much more, as well as every imaginable fusion and mixture between styles and genres.

In this supermarket almost everything is for sale and sometimes the music is free, but usually you have to do something to obtain it (go to a concert, buy a CD, download it and at the very least listen actively). Just as frequently we are confronted with it without asking (on the street, in shops, at the dentist, in the office or other places of work, in an aeroplane). Although no one has requested such a quantity and variety of music, everyone can find something to their liking. Such excess also forces us to choose what we do and do not want to hear. But is this possible? Do we have the correct resources at our disposal for this? Besides, who controls this seemingly free market? Who ultimately decides what can be found on the shelves of the supermarket, what we can hear on the radio, what we can download?

Sometimes it seems as though we the consumers have this power, certainly with new technologies and Internet services. We would then have the complete freedom to consume what we want. But is this the reality? We can of course store and retrieve everything on the Internet. A macroscopic amount of music is divided in this way over what are sometimes microscopic groups of people, right down to a single individual; to just one fan, but at least a fan of your product. This actually suits the function of music as being there for every separate individual, and the way in which we deal with music. Your taste is not the same as mine. Nevertheless, in the world of music, too, we have producers and consumers and, not to forget, a multitude of intermediaries. In particular, we shouldn't lose sight of the complex role of all those producers and middlemen.

Every person brings forth culture, individually or collectively. In principle every person can therefore also produce art, namely art as a product of culture. This is mainly a matter of willingness and ability. Almost every person consumes art as a product of culture. Art as a product often has to take a long journey from the moment of conception to the moment it can be consumed. Numerous interests lie on this journey: the interests of creative artists and of clients, the interests of performing artists who predominantly recreate art, and of intermediaries, organisational bodies, companies and organisations which procure, broadcast or trade in the product. Of course there are also the interests of the consumers, you and me as listeners and art lovers. Each of these interests is again linked to social and economic frameworks within which the relevant artistic expression operates. This is because art in all its manifestations is representative: it represents the society from which it has arisen.

Given that art has a representative function, its creation, production and reproduction as well as its consumption can never be seen as separate from underlying expectations, obligations and desires. And since creative and re-creative artists see their profession as a source of income in much the same way as do bakers or carpenters, lawyers of postmen, art is also merchandise. No 'cultus' without 'pecunia' – or no culture without money, and no pasture without grazing cattle. In Latin the word *cultus* means that which is grown (grasses, grain or crops) or is worshipped, and *pecus* is cattle, which can both be eaten as well as traded – which is why the Latin word for money is *pecunia*. Conversely, the cattle need pasture on which to graze, in order to put enough meat on their bones so that they can be traded. *Pecunia* therefore benefits from *cultus*: the economy benefits from a well-developed culture.

In line with this, we can assume that the artist, if he wants to take his profession seriously, has no other choice than to ensure that he can make his living with his art, if necessary can support his family and, which is not unimportant, can hold a function and position in society. This also means that he must be paid, even if only in kind. Art is a product with a price. But traditionally the consumer has been king, even when it comes to art. He who pays can demand something in return. Kings, prelates, wealthy citizens or whoever it was who paid for art, did so with a strong sense of self-interest until well into the 19th century. After all, art represents as much the commissioner who stands for a society or social class as it does the maker of that art.

In short, art and society are indivisible. The role of art *in* society is at least as essential as art that emerges *from* society. The constant exchange between the two also shows how strong the mutual connection is between individual identity and common identity. The way in which a group of art lovers identifies itself through the art which they consume is largely determined by social factors: their position, education, collective taste and by what they come into contact with on a daily basis. Conversely, however, society is also in part determined by the cultural insights of those who are members of that society. This is why the reception of art, the way in which we interact with and judge art, is closely connected with what is happening in society. This is also why an awareness of this unbreakable relationship is so important both for those who create art as for the consumers, and it is no less important for policy makers.

Western cultural attitudes changed in the course of the 18th and 19th centuries from being mainly ethical into becoming almost entirely aesthetic. The ancient ethical basis of art (art 'is' and art 'must') was therefore exchanged for an aesthetic basis (art 'becomes', perceived in particular as beautiful or exciting). The question as to whether an object of art was beautiful or ugly played a merely secondary role until well into the 18th century. Especially with 'official' art, art that was connected to the community, the direct reason for the commission or the occasion at which the work of art would be unveiled was far more important than its beauty. Everything revolved around utility and purpose.

When in the course of the 18th century – and not only as a result of the philosophical attitude of Kant in his *Kritik der Urteilskraft* – music was entirely removed from the domain of reason and transferred to that of taste and emotion, it turned out to be remarkably difficult to connect music to any other purpose than that of its own beauty. But how could we objectively define the beauty of a work of art? On the basis of taste? Would it even be possible to put a thing like 'taste' into words without being subjective and personal? Despite many extensive and often grandiloquent books and studies, no progress was made. Every reasonable discourse about music on the basis of concepts such as beauty and taste was nullified in no time: all you have is the taste of one person set against that of another. However, people were at least of the opinion that taste could be acquired and developed through education and schooling. A good education would lead to good taste, bearing in mind that this would be the good taste of the higher and well-educated echelons in society. Even the cultivation of good taste cannot conceal that any objective and reasonable assessment is impossible within any aesthetic view of art.

This situation was not made simpler by the 19th century's growing interest in the past, in the music of that past, and thereby the conviction that the works produced by the old masters were an important measure of the quality of contemporary art. On the one hand, any discussion of music at the level of its materials and techniques had become off-limits (since it consists purely of emotions and is not approachable through reason), and on the other hand, music before Haydn and Mozart was taken out of its aesthetic context and, in its elevated and often misunderstood beauty, presented as exemplary against the then new music. After 1850, the newest music became increasingly removed from the general taste of the moneyed classes. In the second half of the 19th century the bourgeoisie sought safe refuge from the rise of modernity, against the music of composers such as Richard Strauss, Mahler, Debussy, Scriabin and Schoenberg, who followed a line influenced by Beethoven's late works and the progressive ideas of composers such as Liszt and Wagner. Their solution was 'old' music: around 1900, for example, the compositions of Bach, but also of Brahms and Tchaikovsky, and later even a lot of earlier music.

After the First World War a new class became a force to be reckoned with, also on the cultural stage: that of the labourers, the proletariat. Just as the middle class before them, they enjoyed more and better education. The market for art and culture therefore grew considerably, certainly after 1945. The music department of the cultural supermarket was successively filled with popular art (initially as an expression of youth culture), improvised music (alongside the other well-known and already established forms of jazz) and all kinds of ethnic music from all over the world. Parallel to this, the market was flooded with a multitude of new carriers for all this valued produce: singles and long-playing records, cassette tapes and CDs, then computers, portable hard drives, MP3 players and now especially the Internet; that wonderful world of the web, with more information at our disposal than anyone has ever had before. The warehouse of contemporary culture has grown so rich that it is impossible for any one person to take everything from it, let alone to study it.

So we have to make choices. These are based on a combination of musical preference and collective identity. As we have already seen above and elsewhere, both of these are to a great extent socially determined, learned, taught, taken on. And time and again, taste plays a significant role in this. What do we consider beautiful, what suits us, what touches us, with what do we want to be identified, to what do we want to belong? It is very rare that we listen to music as a 'must', and at most because it cannot be helped, because we have no alternative. Composers sometimes advance that 'must' as an argument for their choices: it must be so – I can do it no other way. However, they too cannot entirely free themselves from an aesthetic musical judgement.

As a result of this predominant emphasis on aesthetics, music – even more than the visual arts, dance, film or literature – is often merely seen as a 'biscuit to go with the tea', a pleasant addition to our existence, but not a necessity. We haven't really been able to change this since Kant's day. Moreover, many music lovers, performing musicians and concert programmers simply find old music more beautiful than the bulk of contemporary music, since the latter is less mellifluous and less melodious, and with no prior knowledge or experience it also seems less easy to follow. Through repeated performances old music has become better known and therefore increasingly recognisable.

Although contemporary music is a mirror of the world in which we live now, it is at odds with the practical reality. We choose a music that reflects another world, a world as we would like it to be: beautiful, comfortable, snug, and most importantly, not too complex. Just enjoy the music, close your eyes, no need to think at all. For many, music serves above all as an escape from everyday reality.

Many of today's contemporary composers wrestle with these problems. In the 1960s some were already seeking better contact with the public, and wondered if the primary aim of their music should be beauty. But does beauty necessarily mean provided with recognisable melodies and pleasant harmonies, and not being too complicated? For example, it seems that the Dutch national classical radio station (NPO Radio4) has nothing better to offer than slogans based on 'experience and emotion'. Could it be otherwise? During the troubled 1960s, some composers began to quote 'old' music in their new works. Their starting point was mainly to deliver constructive commentary on the high romantic music of Mahler, Strauss, Reger and the young Schoenberg. This was to be an intellectual game with the past, as in fact Stravinsky had done already in his way in his neoclassical works in the 1920s.

Thus, neoromanticism made its appearance almost simultaneously with a new simplicity and a new spirituality, which is often considered to be 'new age', too, and minimal or repetitive music with its references to both manifold ethnic forms of music as well as pop music. 'Let's return to the sources of Western music' was an oft-heard battle cry. Back to the old craft. Sometimes it seems as if during the last decades of the last century, every imaginable style and every imaginable technique was worth a try.

After a 'dip' in the second half of the 20th century, when the complexity and sometimes also the emphatic disharmony and aggressiveness of many a composition went over many people's heads, there are once again contemporary composers who enjoy great popularity and speak to a wide audience. Of these we need only think of Philip Glass and Steve Reich, Arvo Pärt, Tan Dun,

David Del Tredici, Johan Adams, Einojuhani Rautavaara, Simeon ten Holt, Louis Andriessen and Jacob ter Veldhuis (JacobTV). These composers have in common that they create music that is easily followed by less experienced ears, and onto which anyone can project their own narratives and emotions. That is perhaps the great harvest from the last seventy years: we have discovered where the boundaries of listening and of the ability to understand music lie. We have recognised how important it is to reflect on music on the basis of narrative concepts, in order to take audiences on a (thankfully still frequently) unknown journey. To our delight we have found that in the 21st century, too, a large audience will continue to make eager use of the creative artist's generosity.

Everything is now possible and everything is permissible, both in the field of old music as well as the new. Nowadays we know even more about the rules for those countless possibilities, and realise how important it is to master our craft perfectly, certainly compared to those 'oldies' of days long gone. Not so long ago a colleague admitted to me that as a composer, he preferred the situation today to that of around thirty years ago. Back then it was almost impossible to write what you wanted without restrictions. Time and again, you had to account for the reasons for using a certain material, why you applied certain techniques or what your objectives and your artistic points of departure were. Nowadays you can literally write what you want, in every style, on the basis of every technique, with pencil and paper or with the aid of a computer, for an acoustic or an electronic instrumentation, for film, the concert hall or for commercials, with political or purely financial motives, and of course just because as a composer you have pleasure in that for which you have been trained: to create.

With unlimited resources at our disposal we can justifiably say: 'Messieurs faites vos jeux!' This is a game that has no losers. In our defragmented, exploded world, every kind of music has an audience. You only need put your products on the shelves of the (online) department store and put out a sign that it is there.

More and more, it seems that we live in a hall of mirrors like those at a funfair. Each mirror reflects the image of whoever looks into it, but also that of the many other mirrors and everyone who is looking into those, and so on. Moreover, mirrors have a curious attraction for us humans, as do labyrinths. Both are symbols of our age. Wracked by doubt, we search for self-affirmation; for an individual identity amongst the masses, and no less, we look for a way; for the right way to take us out of a tangle of possibilities.

In the last decades we have been unable to discern any main path through that tangle of possibilities, no single direction or vision that can be identified unambiguously as the only correct one. Therefore, we have the impression that no indivisible truth exists: not for the present, nor for the future or even the past. Nor is there one single way of contemplating the world, of practising art and dealing with music, of interpreting or evaluating what we hear, see and read. The resulting doubt is the logical consequence of the ideals that we have cherished for many centuries, of the individualism that we humans have pursued so diligently and for so long. This fragmentation is the most striking in music, that wordless and abstract language.

In addition to this, the usefulness of music eludes us, especially when it produces no hard currency. The meaning of music is sought primarily in the non-material: beauty, emotion, elevation. Music should create repose and relaxation. This is at least the view of the majority of a worldwide audience which consists of an increasing number of enthusiasts who for over a century have been used to measuring the development of music against well-known works of great masters from the distant and recent past. It is apparently also that same part of the public that determines the programming of ensembles, venues and radio through its tastes and preferences. However, that same public, and of course the audiences which have yet to be discovered and generated, is certainly open to new experiences and new confrontations, once the way has been properly shown.

In the other fine arts, we have no problem with taking the public by the hand and providing it with background information, even of the pedantic sort. How different the situation is when it comes to music. Nevertheless, music has an extensive grammar, just as with the language of spoken words, one that is certainly equal to that of painting with its multitude of lines, forms and colours. Music is architecture in sound (and no less three-dimensional in its sonic manifestation). Music is a form of higher mathematics on the one hand, and on the other it can act directly on the body and the soul. I have already highlighted these facets. But we prefer to act as if they play no role or have any importance whatsoever, as if they make no contribution to what music is: the most complex and at the same time the most direct of all arts.

All of this is a result of the double attitude we adopt with regard to music. We want to enjoy it mindlessly and purely through our senses, and therefore not learn too much about it. At the same time, music itself as an art and a craft is anything but composed or intended purely for the senses or for mindless consumption. Initiates often state that the enjoyment of music becomes greater as knowledge about it increases. Unfortunately, the 'facts' that are subsequently provided are often little more than facts about the life of the composer, stories about his difficult existence, the lack of understanding for his art and many other kinds of circumstantial evidence. Rarely do we find a serious examination of the various means used by a composer, that is to say, his materials and techniques. However, when a school class is visiting a museum the children are taught about the brushwork used by the painter, or his colour palette, perspective or language of form with no hesitation.

In short, in the field of music education there is a great deal of catching up to be done, especially if we want to take music seriously as an expression of the human spirit, and to start teaching it at long last as a craft on the basis of the elements of which it consists. In the same way that children learn at a young age to recognise and name colours and forms, numbers and letters, taste and smells or the meaning of words; and in the same way that they learn empirically, or through experience, the difference between the softness of various substances, such as the roughness of sandpaper or the sharpness of a needle. In that way they should also be brought into contact with the world of sounds and rhythms, in order that they can experience the diverse qualities of sounds, and in learning by doing can take control of them. Children are already shown at an early stage how to express themselves in words, images and gestures, and the same should also happen now with sound and music: from the kindergarten to the university; creative, inventive, and based on imagination.

This kind of education – and as far as I am concerned, extended and interwoven with other artistic expressions – has benefit for the total forming of young people. Thanks to its high degree of abstraction music trains our brains, our way of thinking and our memory. It sharpens the ability to associate, develops the imagination and is formative for capabilities in abstract thinking. It is not entirely without reason that music and mathematics are closely connected with each other. The nature of music as an essentially non-verbal means of communication implies that music education also contributes to improved social skills and better understanding between cultures. It goes without saying that such an education should not be one-sidedly about Bach, Mozart or Beethoven. Only a bias-free education that at its heart is not historical, and certainly not Eurocentric, can deliver the desired results. The names of composers or their works are not relevant, but the raw materials of art itself are. This is not about existing systems or methods, but is all about inventive, creative and reflective education.

We still are very far from achieving this. Everyone with open ears, however, must admit that music in all its versatility is deeply rooted in our lives: in concert halls, churches, theatres for opera and musicals, at pop and jazz venues, and via the media both at home and beyond. Nothing therefore stands in the way of making a start with serious education, not only in order to achieve better understanding of the meaning of music, but equally so that we can defend ourselves more effectively against the unsolicited coercion exerted on us by music on the street, via advertising or elsewhere.

The meaning of music lies in its ability to touch us directly at the level of our emotions, in the influence that it can exercise on our imagination, but also in the self-evident way with which it can transmit onto us a feeling of transcendence, of elevation and sometimes almost religious exaltation. Music is extremely suggestive, making it a powerful tool in numerous therapies and, according to some, even an effective medicine against illness. Music is also used in feature films and advertising, since after all, it can change the meaning of what we see, how we experience what we see. However, music is at the same time no less than a multi-layered and abstract construction which we cannot assimilate or comprehend other than with our intellect. The meaning of music is therefore that it has an entirely unique meaning for every person. In short, music affirms us as individuals, as members of a community or culture, and as human beings.

Further Reading

Innumerable books have been written on music in every conceivable language. The following list consists of no more than a selection of the books which have accompanied me, some for decades, some only recently, and which have inspired me in my thoughts on music.

Adorno, Theodor, *Philosophy of New Music*, trans. by Robert Hullot-Kentor (University of Minnesota Press, Minneapolis 2006)

Benjamin, Walter, *The Work of Art in the Age of Mechanical Reproduction*, trans. by J.A. Underwood (Penguin Books, London 2008)

Bernstein, Leonard, *The Joy of Music* (Simon & Schuster, New York 1959)

Bernstein, Leonard, *The Unanswered Question. Six Talks at Harvard* (*Charles Eliot Norton Lectures*) (Harvard University Press, Cambridge 1976)

Cooke, Deryck, *The Language of Music* (Oxford University Press, Oxford 1959)

Copland, Aaron, *What to Listen for in Music* (Whittlesey House, New York 1939; rev. edition Penguin, New York, 1999)

Cowart, Georgia J., *The Triumph of Pleasure, Louis XIV and the Politics of Spectacle* (University of Chicago Press, Chicago 2008)

Goehr, Lydia, *The Imaginary Museum of Musical Works – An Essay in the Philosophy of Music* (Oxford University Press, Oxford 2007)

Guerrieri, Matthew, *The First Four Notes – Beethoven's Fifth and the Human Imagination* (Alfred Knopf, New York 2012)

Honing, Henkjan, *The Illiterate Listener. On Music Cognition, Musicality and Methodology* (Vossiuspers UvA, Amsterdam University Press, Amsterdam 2011)

James, Jamie, *The Music of the Spheres. Music, Science and the Natural Order of the Universe* (Abacus, London 1995)

Kivy, Peter, *Music Alone. Philosophical Reflections on the Purely Musical Experience* (Cornell University Press, Ithaca 1990)

Leppert, Richard and Susan McClary (eds), *Music and Society. The Politics of Composition, Performance and Reception* (Cambridge University Press, Cambridge 1987)

Levitin, Daniel, *This Is Your Brain On Music: The Science of a Human Obsession* (Dutton Penguin, New York 2006)

Meyer, Leonard B., *Emotion and Meaning in Music* (University of Chicago Press, Chicago 1956)

Mithen, Steven, *The Singing Neanderthals – The Origins of Music, Language, Mind and Body* (Harvard University Press, Cambridge 2006)

Nolthenius, Hélène, *Duecento: The Late Middle Ages in Italy* (McGraw-Hill, New York 1968)

Scruton, Roger, *The Aesthetics of Music* (Oxford University Press, Oxford 1979)

Serres, Michel, *Musique* (Éditions Le Pommier, Paris 2011)

Storr, Amthony, *Music and the Mind* (Ballantine Books, New York 1993)

Stravinsky, Igor, *Poetics of Music* (Harvard University Press, Cambridge 1947)

Index of names

Adams, John 52, 229
Adorno, Theodor Wiesengrund 11
Alexakis, Effy 84
Andriessen, Louis 125, 229
Arezzo, Guido of 85
Aristotle 154, 194, 195, 198-201
Aristoxenos 194, 199, 200
Artusi, Giovanni 46, 212
Augustine, Saint 11

Bacchi, Cesare 17
Bach, Carl Philipp Emanuel 210
Bach, Johann Christian 155, 218
Bach, Johann Sebastian 12, 44, 55-75, 77-82, 88, 100, 104, 126, 129, 136, 137, 139, 141, 144, 169, 178, 205, 209, 210, 211, 213-218, 221, 226, 232
Bach, Wilhelm Friedemann 56, 210
Barbireau, Jacques 49
Bartók, Béla 109, 126, 129, 218
Baudelaire, Charles 46
Beatles, The 126
Beauchamps, Pierre de 187
Beethoven, Carl van 118
Beethoven, Ludwig van 9, 11, 22-25, 29, 51, 77, 78, 88, 96, 98, 100, 101, 102, 104-109, 113-124, 125, 126, 128, 129, 136, 138, 139, 141, 154, 155, 162, 163, 165, 169, 174-177, 214-216, 221, 226, 232
Beinum, Eduard van 160
Benserade, Isaac de 187, 190
Berg, Alban 25, 141
Berlin Philharmonic Orchestra 167, 177
Berlioz, Hector 122, 123, 161, 163, 164, 165, 169
Bernadotte, count Jean-Baptiste 115
Bernstein, Leonard 11, 165
Berwald, Franz 129
Bettenhaussen, Michel 158
Beurden, Bernard van 10
Bingen, Hildegard von 220
Binkley, Thomas 218, 219
Bonaparte, Jérôme 116, 118
Bonaparte, Joseph 118
Bonaparte, Napoléon 116, 117, 118, 119, 213
Boulez, Pierre 42, 88, 125, 126, 129, 139, 144, 165
Bourgeois, Louise 104

Bowie, David 126
Brahms, Johannes 23, 25, 107, 109, 123, 126, 129, 144, 156-158, 169, 215, 218, 226
Brautigam, Ronald 175
Brel, Jacques 46, 51
Brendel, Alfred 103, 176, 177
Britten, Benjamin 144
Brubeck, Dave 152, 153
Bruch, Max 152
Bruckner, Anton 22, 23, 25, 91-94, 144, 215
Brüggen, Frans 178, 218
Bülow, Hans von 166, 168, 169
Burney, Charles 208, 209, 210
Busoni, Ferruccio 213, 214
Buti, Francesco 190
Byrd, William 154, 204

Cabezón, Antonio de 154, 155
Cambefort, Jean de 187, 191
Cape, Safford 9
Caproli, Carlo 190
Castiglioni, Baldassare 185
Cavalli, Francesco 191
Celibidache, Sergiu 91, 171
Charles II, King of England 190
Cherubini, Luigi 122, 155
Chladenius, Johann Martin 205
Chopin, Frédéric 56, 73, 78, 102, 103, 129, 173
Christoffersen, Peter Woetmann 210
Ciccolini, Aldo 104
Ciconia, Johannes 129
Claudius Ptolemaeus 199
Clemencic, René 219
Clementi, Muzio 74, 176
Cohen, Leonard 46
Concertgebouw Orchestra 176, 218
Confucius (Kong Qui, Kongzi) 34
Copernicus, Nicolaus 67, 68
Corelli, Archangelo 204
Cowen, Frederic 151
Cromwell, Oliver 190
Czerny, Carl 56, 59, 60, 74, 114

De Laborde, Jean-Benjamin 208
Debussy, Claude 51, 74, 88, 126, 139, 144, 169, 226

Dolmetsch, Arnold 178
Dolmetsch, Carl 178
Dowland, John 155
Dufay, Guillaume 144, 154, 155
Dvořák, Antonín 149-155
Dylan, Bob 46

Eisler, Hanns 79
Epicure 194, 199, 200
Escher, Rudolf 27, 131-133, 168

Ferguson, Marijke 10
Fischer, Johann Caspar Ferdinand 56, 68
Forkel, Johann Nikolaus 208-212, 216
Framéry, Nicolas-Étienne 208
Franck, César 29
Freud, Sigmund 97
Furtwängler, Wilhelm 165, 167, 171
Fux, Johann Joseph 205, 207, 212

Gabrieli, Giovanni 214
Geminiani, Francesco 212
Gerbert, Martin 208, 212
Gissey, Henri de 188
Glass, Philip 228
Glaucon 196
Gluck, Christoph Willibald von 218
Goethe, Johann Wolfgang von 46-47, 153, 154, 205
Gogh, Vincent van 132
Gossec, François-Joseph 115
Gounod, Charles 73, 74
Grandville, Jean J. 164
Gregory I, Pope 18, 35-36, 135
Grétry, André 115
Grieg, Edvard 77, 150, 151
Groot, Cor de 9
Guerrieri, Matthew 138

Habeneck, François-Antoine 163
Hagen, Nina 126
Haitink, Bernard 176
Händel, Georg Friedrich 165, 215
Hanslick, Eduard 82, 83
Harnoncourt, Nikolaus 178
Hassler, Hans Leo 179
Hawkins, John 208, 212
Haydn, Joseph 67, 74, 96, 98, 105-108, 125-128, 132, 141, 155, 169, 174, 215, 216, 218, 226
Hayter, George 161
Heine, Heinrich 21

Heksch, Alice 9
Hellmesberger, Joseph 107
Hiller, Johann Adam 213
Hindemith, Paul 88, 135, 136, 139, 178
Hoffmann, Ernst Theodor Amadeus 47, 105, 128
Holt, Simeon ten 144, 229
Homer 34
Honegger, Arthur 140
Honing, Henkjan 32
Hubermann, Bronislav 100
Hüttenbrenner, Anselm 18

Ibsen, Henrik 77
Isaac, Heinrich 208

James II, King of England 189, 190
Jeunesse Musicale 10
Joachim, Joseph 107
Jochum, Eugen 91
Joseph II, Emperor 176

Kant, Immanuel 11, 47, 95, 96, 103, 105, 108, 109, 200, 206, 225
Karajan, Herbert von 171, 177
Keilberth, Joseph 160
Kempf, Wilhelm 175
Kepler, Johannes 66, 68
Keuris, Tristan 144
Kinsky, Prince Ferdinand 118
Kirnberger, Johann Philipp 212
Klemperer, Otto 89
Klijn, Nap de 9
Kloos, Willem 109
Kodály, Zoltán 218
Koos, Dr. Geza de 100
Korngold, Erich 98
Kuhnau, Johann 80

Lambert, Michel 187
Landowska, Wanda 178
Lang Lang 103
Langer, Susanne K. 93, 97
Lassus, Orlande de 22, 214
Le Brun, Charles 192
Le Nôtre, André 192
Leeuw, Reinbert de 104
Leeuw, Ton de 220
Leibniz, Gottfried Wilhelm von 37
Leonhardt, Gustav 178
Lesueur, Jean-François 122, 123
Levi, Hermann 168, 169
Ligeti, Gyögy 82

237

Lipatti, Dinu 175
Liszt, Ferenc (Franz) 88, 159, 215, 226
Lobkowitz, Prince Franz Joseph Maximilian von 118
Longfellow, Henry Wadsworth 151
Louis XIII 186, 191
Louis XIV, King of France 185-193
Lucretius 199
Lully, Jean-Baptiste 160, 188-193
Lustig, Wilhelm 212

MacDowell, Edward 150, 151, 152, 154
Machaut, Guillaume de 9, 22, 42, 129, 144
Mahler, Gustav 25, 29, 44, 82, 88, 129, 136, 143, 165, 167-169, 171, 176, 214, 215, 221, 226, 228
Maintenon, Françoise d'Aubigné, marquise de 190
Malibran, Maria 159
Marez Oyens, Tera de 10
Marpurg, Friedrich 206, 212
Martini, Giovanni Battista 206, 207
Mattheson, Johann 56
Mayrhofer, Johann 21
Mazarin, Cardinal Jules Raymond 185-187, 190-193
Méhul, Étienne Nicolas 155
Meijer, Leonard B. 98
Mendelssohn, Felix 106, 161, 162, 163, 169, 213
Mengelberg, Willem 169, 171, 176, 214
Menuhin, Hepzibah 9
Menuhin, Yehudi 9
Mersenne, Marin 66, 71, 72, 208, 212
Messiaen, Olivier 172, 181
Michelangelo Buonarroti 104
Minchin, Tim 46
Mithen, Steven 32
Mitropoulos, Dimitri 160
Molière (Jean-Baptiste Poquelin) 192
Mollier, Louis de 187
Monteverdi, Claudio 22, 46, 48, 78, 79, 126, 139, 141, 144, 159, 174, 179, 215, 221
Morales, Cristobal de 179
Moscheles, Ignaz 117, 162
Moses 135
Moskowski, Moritz 151
Mottl, Felix 160
Mozart, Constanze 142
Mozart, Leopold 45, 96, 145, 212
Mozart, Maria Anna (Nannerl) 138

Mozart, Wolfgang Amadeus 9, 11, 22, 23, 29, 42, 44, 45, 51, 67, 74, 78, 88, 96, 106, 107, 115, 117, 125-129, 132, 136-139, 141, 142, 144, 145, 155, 162, 169, 175, 176, 178, 206, 207, 213, 215-218, 226, 232

Nikisch, Arthur 168, 169
North, Roger 204

Obrecht, Jacob 28
Ockeghem, Johannes 28, 208, 209, 210
Otten, Willem Jan 10
Otterloo, Willem van 166

Pachelbel, Johann 218
Paganini, Niccolò 159, 173
Palestrina, Giovanni Pierluigi da 22, 28, 48, 82, 126, 129, 179, 204, 205, 207, 214, 215, 216
Pärt, Arvo 74, 144, 228
Patti, Adelina 159
Paul, Grand Duke of Russia 176
Pepusch, John Christopher 204
Perahia, Murray 175
Persimfans Orchestra 170
Philipe, Gérard 9
Pires, Maria João 175
Plato 33, 39-40, 108, 153, 154, 194-203
Pollini, Maurizio 102, 103
Praetorius, Michael 179
Prez, Josquin des 22, 28, 88, 126, 129, 139, 141, 144, 174
Pro Musica Antiqua 9
Puccini, Giacomo 44
Purcell, Henry 22, 42, 78, 126, 141, 144, 204
Pyrrho 200
Pythagoras 67, 68, 194-196, 199-201

Rachmaninoff, Sergei 29, 99, 100, 175
Rameau, Jean-Philippe 72
Rameau, Pierre 185
Rautavaara, Einojuhani 229
Ravel, Maurice 44, 129
Razumovsky, count Andreas 106
Reeser, Eduard 218
Reger, Max 9, 228
Reich, Steve 144, 228
Reichardt, Johann Friedrich 117
Rellstab, Ludwig 107
Rembrandt van Rijn 215
Residentie Orchestra The Hague 156-158

Richafort, Jean 129
Richter, Hanns 168, 169
Rorem, Ned 47
Rosa Spier Huis 11
Rosen, Charles 128
Rousseau, Jean-Jacques 207, 212
Rudolph of Austria, archduke 118

Saint-Hubert, Monsieur de 186
Salieri, Antonio 20, 46, 117
Salonen, Esa-Pekka 166
Satie, Erik 104
Sauveur, Joseph 66, 71, 72, 208
Scheibe, Johann Adolf 104, 212
Schein, Johann Hermann 218
Schickele, Peter (P.D.Q. Bach) 113
Schindler, Anton 114
Schnabel, Artur 176
Schober, Franz von 21
Schoenberg, Arnold 25, 88, 109, 125, 226, 228
Schopenhauer, Arthur 11, 35, 108, 109
Schubart, Christian 21
Schubert, Franz 17-26, 35, 42, 51, 73, 108, 117, 129, 136, 137, 144, 215
Schumann, Robert 23, 29, 78, 108, 123, 161, 169, 213, 214
Schuppanzigh, Ignaz 106, 107
Schütz, Heinrich 144, 179, 215
Scriabin, Alexander 226
Seidl, Anton 166, 168
Sextus Empiricus 200
Simmias 195
Sinopoli, Giuseppe 160, 166
Smetana, Bedrich 43, 98
Socrates 195, 196, 197, 200
Spohr, Louis 106, 108, 161
Steen, Jac. van 158
Stenhammar, Wilhelm 129
Stockhausen, Karlheinz 82
Stokowski, Leopold 160, 214
Strauss, Richard 51, 77, 79, 88, 98, 142, 165, 168, 169, 226, 228
Stravinsky, Igor 28, 29, 76-78, 81, 88, 89, 125, 141, 144, 165, 180, 228

Streisand, Barbra 51, 126
Studio der frühen Musik 218, 219
Sulzer, Johann Georg 105
Svetlanov, Evgeni 157
Sweelinck, Jan Pieterszoon 217

Tallis, Thomas 179, 204
Tan Dun 228
Tausig, Carl 166
Tchaikovsky, Pyotr Ilyich 22, 96, 157, 169, 180, 226
Thurber, Jeanette 150
Tilgner, Victor 127
Titian (Tiziano Vecellio) 215
Toscanini, Arturo 167, 168, 169, 171
Tredici, David del 229

Vaqueiras, Raimbaut de 219
Veen, Herman van 51
Veldhuis, Jacob ter 229
Ventadorn, Bernart de 173, 218
Verdi, Giuseppe 22, 42, 51, 141
Vermeulen, Matthijs 109
Victoria, Tomás Luis de 179, 207
Vries, Theun de 28

Wagner, Richard 29, 77, 78, 82, 88, 139, 141, 160-162, 165, 167-169, 171, 226
Watteau, Jean Antoine 206
Webber, Andrew Lloyd 51
Weber, Carl Maria von 108, 161, 165, 169, 215
Webern, Anton 25, 126, 144
Weelkes, Thomas 179
Weingartner, Felix 165, 166
Wellington, Duke of (Arthur Wellesley) 118
Werckmeister, Andreas 66, 70, 72, 75, 212
Winckelmann, Johann Joachim 205
Winehouse, Amy 52

Yinon, Israel 160

About the author

Leo Samama (b. 1951) graduated from the University of Utrecht in Musicology and studied composition for some years under Rudolf Escher. In 1976-77 he continued his doctoral studies at UCLA in Los Angeles, California, supported by a Rotary Foundation Grant. Between 1977 and 1988 Leo Samama taught History of Music and Culture (History of Art, Philosophy and Aesthetics) at the Utrecht Conservatory. Between 1987 and 1989 he lectured on 'Musical criticism in theory and practice' at the Royal Conservatory in The Hague. He worked at the Musicology Department at the Utrecht University between 1988 and 1992, specialising in the Music of the Twentieth Century and Musical Criticism.

Between 1978 and 1984 he was a critic for *de Volkskrant* and between 1986 and 1990 he was a correspondent for *NRC Handelsblad,* both leading newspapers in the Netherlands. He also wrote for several prominent magazines. From 1988 to 1994, Leo Samama sat on the board of the Royal Concertgebouw Orchestra Amsterdam as the orchestra's artistic advisor, and between 1991 and 1993 he was head of the orchestra's artistic department. From 1988 to 1993, Samama was artistic adviser to the Centrum Nederlandse Muziek, an organisation specialising in the promotion of Dutch music. He was an advisor to the NCRV broadcasting company between 1992 and 1994.

From 1994 to 2003, Leo Samama was head of the artistic department of the Residentie Orchestra The Hague, and he was general manager of the Netherlands Chamber Choir between 2003 and 2010. He is the co-founder of the Netherlands String Quartet Academy, and he has given radio broadcasts and guest lectures all over the country.

His musicological writings include books and essays on contemporary music, the philosophy of music and Dutch music in particular. Among his publications are *Nederlandse muziek in de 20-ste eeuw* (*Dutch Music in the 20th Century*, Amsterdam 1986/2006, the first comprehensive survey of the subject), the monograph *Alphons Diepenbrock, componist van het vocale* (*Alphons Diepenbrock, Composer of the Vocal,* Amsterdam, 2012), and *Een beknopt overzicht van duizend jaar Britse muziek* (*A concise survey of 1000 years of British music*, Amsterdam, 2003).

Since 1975 Leo Samama has written some ninety compositions for a great diversity of ensembles, which have been performed all over the world, recorded on CD and broadcast nationally. In the Netherlands, many of his university lectures have been recorded and released on CD. In 2010 Leo Samama was knighted as an Officer of the Order of Orange-Nassau for his contribution to Dutch musical life.

March 2015